MASTERS' TALES *of* NOW

Presenters: Jeshua, Saint Germain, God & Mother Mary, Lord of Justice, AA Michael, Djwhal Khul, Lady Nada, Master Jonas, Serapis Bey, and Kuan Yin.

VERLING CHAKO PRIEST, PH.D.

Order this book online at www.trafford.com
or email orders@trafford.com

Most Trafford titles are also available at major online book retailers.

Cover layout by Susan O'Brien and Jason Smallwood. Photo was taken by Jason in
Paradise Island, Nassau, 2012 from the balcony of the family's condo on the 17th
floor of The Reefs Hotel. Susan cropped the photo and put in the graphics.

Printed in the United States of America.

ISBN: 978-1-4907-1351-9 (sc)
ISBN: 978-1-4907-1350-2 (hc)
ISBN: 978-1-4907-1352-6 (e)

Library of Congress Control Number: 2013915978

Trafford rev. 08/30/2013

 www.trafford.com

North America & international
toll-free: 1 888 232 4444 (USA & Canada)
fax: 812 355 4082

Align us with

SOURCE and the NOW, oh Lord!

I dedicate Book 11 to humanity.

TABLE OF CONTENTS

PREFACE

DREAM: *I heard my FAX machine click on. I went to it and there was a blue colored paper with the Star of David up in the left-hand corner of the page.* End . . . 04-13-13.

I knew the Star represented Jesus, so I spoke to him telepathically as to the meaning of the dream. It was to signify that in a few weeks I would be starting to write a new book (no co-author) set up in a similar fashion as my previous books are. He would be bringing forth Masters who would present their thoughts pertaining to a certain subject. *The main thrust of the dream was to alert you that I (Jeshua) would be coming soon to start another book with you. It is not to take anything away from* JESUS: My Beloved Connection to Humanity and the Sea *that you co-authored with Rev. Cynthia Williams. Your new book will be entirely different with a couple of Masters you never have heard of before.*

Every Saturday I telepathically connect with Jeshua at 2:00 PM. About a month later on May 11th, he greeted me with *Dearest one, we have exciting news for you. We will be starting our new book in two weeks!* A quick look at my calendar showed me that the date would be Saturday, May 25, 2013. I asked for the title, knowing he probably would not give it to me, and sure enough, he said, *not yet, for you know the title comes a little later. We need to see how the translation is coming along first.*

Saint Germain once told me that when people channel, there is a translation that takes place. The Entities that are speaking to us by thought use the Library of our minds to make a translation as to what is said. It is done in an instant. Therefore, Jeshua needed to see how that was coming along before giving a title to the information. In other words, if the information that a Master is attempting to bring forth were for a physicist's mind, my mind would not carry the correct terminology. The translation would have to be simplified or not at all, therefore.

Instead of having a *Prologue*, I took an author's privilege and titled that section *Pre-Rambles*. I think it describes those pages well.

You will find that the *Acknowledgments* section is at the end of the book. Since this is my 11th book, I just wanted to turn the format around a little—show some flexibility and willingness to change.

The title also is a play on words in that so many of us have read *The Brothers Grimm's Fairy Tales*. Well, these tales from the Masters are true stories depicting what is NOW and when the characters are not in the NOW. It is hoped that parents and/ or relatives and friends will read these stories to those unable to read—little children and/or those unable to read any more due to infirmities—so that they will have a better grasp of NOW energy. Being in the NOW is action with no action—no past or future thoughts. It just is. And, of course, any judgments take one out of the NOW.

The original title was *NOW Energy for Now and Forever.* I felt it did not depict the fact that each chapter is a tale, so I changed it to *MASTERS' TALES of NOW.*

PRE-RAMBLES

God bless these words I am hearing and let them be the
spoken Truth from your sons and daughters of Light.
Send us your protection and keep me in your Grace—in
the Christ Light, Amen, Amen, Amen.

"I now demand in the name of Jesus the Christ to know
if you are a Being of the Jesus the Christ Consciousness;
if you are a Being of the true God of the God Light
Consciousness of the Creator, answer me *yes* or *no*."*

Good morning, precious one, this is an auspicious beginning for
our new book. *Good morning, Lord; I need to check you out. (I*
state the above paragraph.) Yes, beloved, it is I, your brother,
Jesus/Jeshua/Sananda, and many other names. You have asked for
a prayer to say before you start on the book each day; the one you
just said is fine. I think I gave you that a long time ago. *Yes.*

Now you have some questions you wish to ask? *Well, this is*
kind of left-brain, but do you wish to get right into the Introduction
or to continue on this Pre-Rambles, as I have called it? Let
us continue here for a while. You have asked for the *reason* and

purpose for the book. It is to bring people closer to the Truth and to get them out and away from so much of their belief systems in the Old Time Religions. As you know, I so wish for people to just be in their hearts and not worry so much as to the old Biblical sayings. I know that the Bible is still revered, and rightly so. I also know that there were misinterpretations from the scribes, and so the words became garbled. I am hoping people can let go of some of that programming.

The purpose, therefore, is to bring people into present time—to get them away from those belief systems of 2000+ years ago. The religions are not making it easy, since so many of the preachers use the same material over and over again. Nothing seems to move forward. They are always taking a saying and attempting to get new interpretations from it. This needs to change, for it keeps them perpetually in the same groove . . . over and over in a rut—a circular rut.

The Catholic Church is a good example. I know there are millions of Catholics, and those teachings bring them solace, but they do not understand that they need to move on—get a new perspective. Having the masses in Latin all the time does not help. People in modern times do not know that language and so are apt to just doze through it all. The idea of having to go to a priest for ablution is also not correct, so there needs to be much change. Questions for me? *Of course, I would like the title of this book.* And we are not quite ready to give it to you yet . . . all in good time, dear one.

Would you describe your process in coming to me on an energy band? How far—to my mental body, etc. Please explain. Since you have stepped into another dimension, I am able to come closer. I come as Sananda now, but many still will feel me as Jesus. However, I come to your highest mental body and speak to you by thought. You make the translation in your scribing—we connect through your heart and the higher mind. While you were getting ready to channel a while ago, you felt me in your heart and felt tearful, plus your body had goose bumps, telling you a Being was close by. I do not enter your body per se, as you are not a full body channel, but the energies that I pour into your body would not be acceptable for others; let us say it would overpower them for they would not be able to take that level of energy.

Now, dear one, let us switch gears here unless you have some more questions. *I wish to know if we are going to have our little conversations before and after a Presenter like we have done in the past.* There may be times I make comments, but it is not that kind of a book, so just the Presenter will speak in each chapter. 5-25-13

Author: I have noticed that as I progressed through the chapters, the Presenters and Jeshua were making personal comments. I did not edit those out, thinking they may be of interest to the reader. 8-14-13.

*   *Readers, you will find this and other Commands from Sananda in the Appendix.*

INTRODUCTION

Beloveds, I am Jesus/Sananda, coming to you today to bring you a new concept that will be for this new book. The subject matter will be a philosophical one, for we will discuss the Father's world. We will discuss what it means to be in present time—the NOW. So, without further adieu, I shall begin. 5-25-13

In the Heavenly Realms, there is a band of energy that has no motion and yet it is not static. It is an area of total peace, love, allowing, and letting go—no control. The Being comes for rejuvenation, which can take several millions of years, for there is no linear time as you perceive it. It is the Monad that brings its pieces or fingers of energies together and then enters this quiet sanctuary.

This time also becomes an opportunity for contemplation. The soul has total memory of all of its journeys and so it becomes a time to thumb through its memory book to see what could have been improved and what needs to be adjusted or whether it needs to repeat a life in order to glean what that was all about.

When the soul feels finished with its contemplation, it has a choice to either stay put for another million years or so, to seek new worlds to explore, or to go back to Earth and get involved in some new way. You may be thinking or asking yourself, how does that play into staying in the NOW? I/we (for I am never alone) understand how that can be confusing, but to simplify it, think of just being in present time. You are in the NOW at every moment then.

Let us move on to another thought. Many people think that they are in present time when they are just doing a bodily act like going to the store. However, their mind is not particularly thinking about the store, but rather what's for dinner, when to pick up the kids, what movies to see that night. Time-wise, you may think you are in present time, but your mind is not. It can be on another planet, checking out those dynamics. **Thinking and doing are two different realities.**

Let us pick up the pace a bit, and we suggest you try to remain thinking about vegetables as you are grocery shopping or thinking about the children's activities as you pick them up. It has to do with action and mind in sync. When there is that synchronicity, there can be NOW energy.

The NOW energy has many variations to it. Many Lightworkers have their own take on it, but we in the Heavenlies particularly think of it as being ever present, no linear time, simply as is—what is, is; what was, was. NOW is at what is, is. And there is no judgment.

For many years, aeons ago, people stayed pretty much in the NOW. I know this may sound incredulous to many of you. But you see, life was so simple back then. It was not complicated by television, newspapers, magazines, cell phones, Internet games, texting, and photos. All of that has come into the present and has created its source of chaos. There is no chaos when you are in the NOW. There is simplicity: what is, is.

You may be surprised to know that when people are out on the battlefields, there can be the NOW. When soldiers are dying, they are in the NOW. When the angels appear to lead the soul Home, they are in the NOW. **NOW is action of no action.** Do you understand? Just as you have heard when someone says he/ she is not going to make a choice, that then becomes a choice in itself—not to make a choice. The NOW energy is similar in that it is simple; it is NOW—no effort, no control—it is NOW.

This channel (Chako), hearing my thoughts as I come into her mental body, is in the NOW. She hears the birds chirping, for she sits in the alcove in her bedroom looking out on the lemon tree— Morning Doves cooing back and forth. However, she still is in the NOW. She is sitting with her eyes closed at this point, allowing me to come ever closer, allowing her energy to arise to meet me. We are both connecting at a very high level, and we are in the NOW.

I believe one of the problems that people have stems from the fact that they tend to make it more complicated than it is. Their left brain gets in the way and they try to figure it out from the mental body. That is not the NOW; it is merely the ego with its energies of control. But when one is in the heart, the silence of the heart, everything is in the NOW. It is what it is.

Aeons ago, as I was saying, although life was harsh, it was still simplistic. A person arose from his/her night's sleep; if there were water close by, water was splashed on the face. If there were a twig handy, the twig was dipped into the water and run over the teeth. If there were apples nearby, the person would reach up and pick an apple with thanks and chew breakfast. Simple.

I have much that I wish to say to you, but I need to take you way back to antiquity. While I come from those Biblical times, from what you call Israel, I am also speaking of Egypt, Greece, and before that, Atlantis, and before that, Lemuria. Let yourself go back to those ancient times and see and feel how simplistic life was. People did not think that much philosophically. They were into the body requests—foods, drink, sex, sleep, evacuate the bowels—simplistic.

There were great Thinkers, as you know, but dark was upon the planet. There was discord, and that caused disruptions to the NOW. People were scattered in their minds. They were thinking of many things—usually security, or how to take revenge, or how to obtain someone else's wealth, or how to obtain someone else's woman or man. They lost their values because they were in survival. They were not even in present time; they were self-centered, what psychologists would call *narcissistic*. Almost every act that was taken pertained to that person—*I'm so hungry; I've got to have something to eat*—then he/she would grab or steal anything from a vendor. There was little philosophy of moral teachings.

The religions came through, eating away the perimeters of any energy of self-value that was still present. It is most difficult to be in that higher vibration of the NOW when you are being fed the lies, the distortions, the control of the different religions. There is no NOW when you are heavily into the religions. Fundamentalists are always espousing this and that, most of it not Truth. There is no NOW then.

Coming forward from those ancient times, the great philosophers (Aristotle for one, Plato, may not have been totally correct) were tuning into the higher vibration and were touching the NOW. Even then, they could not totally immerse themselves in it.

One may be asking that when the NOW is so allusive, why is it so important to be attempting to manifest it in the present? Why bother? Because humanity is evolving. The souls are wishing to re-establish their connections with the Creator. They are remembering what it is like to rest so lovingly and peacefully in that NOW energy that I have told you about. This is what they are seeking. This is what they are attempting to bring forth once again—to be aligned with Source.

Beloveds, now is the time to find that part of you that remembers the NOW. It is time to reconnect with that part of you—to bring yourself to higher and higher levels in your journey back to God, back to Source.

Dear ones, I will ask you to turn the page so that we can start our first chapter and give you further ideas about the NOW.

1

COUNT SAINT GERMAIN

Good day to you, my precious one. I am known as Saint Germain. I have come to you many times before.

We come this day to give you different perspectives, so I will add a story that will describe what we have been referring to when speaking of the NOW.

Many years ago, when I was a young Count, I spent my time in the houses of royalty. It was a boisterous time—a gluttonous time—where people were into their orgies. Platters of food were served. Nowadays, you would be aghast—not just 3 courses, but 10 courses—a whole roast pig, a whole roast lamb, whole pheasants, even little ducklings were presented as a delicacy—anything to jaw on. It was a culinary delight to see how the food was decorated. The feathers were stuck back into the foul so that the birds would look alive. A piglet would have an apple in its mouth. And on it went—glorious presentations of food—platter after platter.

Meanwhile, drinks were served—various wines and beers of different flavors, different preparations, and different malts. Some of the wines sparkled; some did not. All the Lords and Ladies were dressed—overdressed. It could be very warm in the summertime, and they were always overdressed with their corsets—even some of the men wore corsets to help put their paunch back into place. There were no deodorants, as you know, way back then. Therefore, the perfumes had to be heavily sprinkled on the bodies to mask the odors.

The heavy gowns of velvets were not washed that frequently. In fact many of them never were washed. There were no dry-cleaning systems, so the maids just beat the dust out of them. They would take a dab of water on a cloth and rub some of the stains out as best they could.

The clothes were covered in jewels. If there was grease spattered on one, a huge stone pin could be put in place to hide the problem.

Therefore, you had the gluttony of eating. Then you had the gluttony of over-furbishing your body with the heavy clothing. On top of that was the gluttony of jewels that loaded down your frame, worn to hide many imperfections.

People did not recognize personal boundaries. There was flirting, going beyond flirting, always finding ways to get into someone else's bed. The spouses people were married to usually came from arranged marriages. Few would love each other, but one would have more money; one would be more beautiful. They were marriages of contract and conveniences. But of course there was love, but love was usually beyond reach. Consequently, they had all of these assignations for people wanting to get together.

The energies of the halls were chaotic, for you had again the gluttony of foods; the gluttony of draped bodies in ostentatious finery; the gluttony of energies with sexual intonations. If a person was gay, and many of royalty were, there would be the simpering of the gay men, copying women's ways of stance and being to make themselves more attractive to one of the same sexual orientation. There was gluttony in sexual preferences also. There was no NOW energy. There was no love and peace and non-judgment, only chaos. Can you imagine going to a meal that never started until 10:00 at night and stuffing yourself in all ways—the gluttony of over-eating—the chaos? All was so chaotic. Keep in mind these are the royals I am describing.

Of course, I was a Count; I was playing the game. I too dressed outrageously. But the difference was I knew it! I knew why I did it; I played their game. It was not my intention to out-do anyone else as so many of my companions did. I retained the consciousness of what I was doing. I attempted in my own way to direct people's energies. As you know, you cannot change anyone. You only can direct energy. I tried in vain to help some of the royals who would not listen and got their heads chopped off. I tried in vain to direct them into other ways of being.

All this gluttony and chaos was going on in these magnificent buildings. Those of you who have visited the Palace of Versailles know what I mean.

While all of this was playing out with the royals, the common people were going through the garbage trying to find a crust of bread. The plague struck, for they did not know it came from the fleas on rats that roamed the streets.

Where was the NOW? There was none. Some of it was in present time, as a person lay dying from the plague.

I give you this little story so you will have a behind—the-scenes idea of those gluttonous times that perhaps you had not read in history books. Of course, there were some who were in their hearts. That was more often found out on the farms where a child held new baby chicks, or the wife helped a new lamb to nurse. There was love where the air was free, for nothing else was. The people were heavily taxed which led to cheating and trying not to give what was being asked of them—always scrambling for survival.

Many souls made contracts to come in to experience those times. There was so much learning available for souls. So if you find out about some past lives where you were a royal princess or even a queen or king, just know that one of the reasons you chose that lifetime was for the learning experience of what it would be like to be a glutton.

As we look at TV reality shows, there is one about *hoarding*. The camera shows these people almost buried under all their hoarded stuff. It is not satins, jewels and furs; it is just stuff—the soul remembering and not being able to leave behind that energy of being a glutton in a past-life game. It brought it all forth into this lifetime; the soul still needs much inner work in order to make that distinction and to see the lessons that were provided and to let go of that hoarding energy.

These souls who are hoarders are a prime example for humanity. Picture those people in the royalty times of France—I know similar games were being played in other countries, but since I was in France, I speak of the French royals. Think of those people who are hoarding now and what it would be like back then. They were gluttons in everything they did, and so now in present times, the souls have brought that entire energy forward, not being able to let it go. Deep past-life regression would help them, but they would have to make the effort to delve into that. Sometimes the pain of having to give up all of their possessions is too tremendous, for they have not done that inner clearing where they can let go. There is no NOW in any of those situations.

I leave you now, but I wish to give you this thought. Where is it in your life that you are in the NOW energy? When is it that you feel such peace and love and quietness, for then you are thoroughly immersed in the NOW energy. Try to pinpoint that in your life and bring more of that forward, because when you do, you are remembering the NOW, the Creator's NOW, the exquisiteness of having nothing to do. And yet, the time (no linear time) seems filled. There is no boredom; you are just filled with love and contemplation.

Dear friends, it is always a joy to be in one of Chako's books. I love her dearly. She, Jeshua, and I ride tandem on a bicycle, which

I often have told her. She steers; we ride the back pedals, but we are always with her. Sometimes she wonders, for she is a telepathic channel versus a direct voice, full body channel. She thinks once in a while how wonderful it would be to be a voice channel and have Saint Germain emit the sounds and to feel his energy. But I can guarantee when I am this close, she is feeling me.

I bless her with the violet flame as it covers her and the book with blessings.

I AM Saint Germain

All right, dear one, that is it for today. I hope you enjoyed that, and we thank you for bringing in this information so clearly. Until we meet again tomorrow (5-27-13).

I AM Jeshua.

2

GOD & MOTHER MARY

Hello my beloved, I AM your **Mother/Father God**. (*Oh, how wonderful!*) I come this morning to add My perspective to what the NOW is all about. When the soul comes into My territory, it comes almost like a weary traveler. It is seeking solace from the troubles of the worlds it has been visiting and involving itself with. It has been millions of years since it had last visited this oasis—this NOW. Think of it as a *weary traveler* having to solve problems, having to find places to rest, having to work with families, having to jiggle and juggle energies. It takes its toll so that there becomes a pull whereby the Monad gathers up all of its strings of consciousness and says, *enough already! I am going Home for a while*. And he/she comes with his entire family.

He does actually leave one string outside of the NOW so that he can find his way out to another world. Once you are in the NOW energy, you do not want to leave, so souls stay and stay, rejuvenate and relax, get their bearings again and look over their long past journey—the pros and cons of it.

In this NOW energy, you have been told there is peace. This peace is something that you, beloved readers, have never experienced in this lifetime, for it is only available in the NOW— this deep peace and the deep love that goes with it.

Souls tremble when they feel that little tug from the string of consciousness they have left outside the parameter. *OK, time to go back to work.*

It sounds like they are taking a long nap, as if they are wasting time. But you see, dearly beloveds, you are thinking in linear time. In My world of the NOW, time actually does not exist. It just is. The passing of years, the passing of centuries, the passing of cycles—the soul really does not know—for it just basks in the wonderful energy that I provide for it, feeling love, feeling safe, feeling at Home.

There is not much more that I can say at this time for this is a difficult concept to grasp. Let it soak in; let it jell; remember; remember what it is like to be Home.

I bless you, My dear children; I see every struggle; I see your baby steps forward and the tumbling backwards. I hear your cries, just like a parent and the toddler. You are My children and I dearly love you. I am always here for you; I am in your heart.

I AM Father/Mother God.

(All right, dear one, the Father wished to say a few words for it allowed His energy to permeate the book so that those who are reading the book will feel His love and His peace. Maybe that is all they will need to do—just feel Him. We now have another Master that will step forth. It is a woman this time, and I will let her introduce herself.)

MOTHER MARY

Hello everyone, beloved readers, I AM called Mother Mary, or you can just call me *Mary*. I have known this channel for aeons of time. She was my daughter (*Mariam*) whom I had adopted way back when Yeshua was young. They had such a connection; they knew each others' thoughts and literally grew up with each other. They then went their separate ways and for this channel into different lifetimes. Now here she is a senior, an advanced senior with an advanced consciousness and developed abilities to bring in this work.

We are talking about the NOW. I, myself, have basked in that energy—the Father's energy. I was there for a million years or so. You did not know me then, but I did experience it, and I will be going back one of these days, but not for a while.

I wish to tell you a story—one of my past lives—that may give you an inkling of what we are talking about. I was born into a very wealthy family. (I will not describe it more than that.) One parent loved me but the other parent was too busy—my father. I am sure he loved me in his own way, but he had a difficult time showing it.

It was an era of linear time when parents sent their children away from home at a very early age to be educated. Therefore, the child actually was molded by its teachers' influence—teachers' consciousness. Or its teachers' unconsciousness! The teachers were very strict. They had their own way of doing things, of controlling, and the punishments were very severe.

Imagine a five year old being sent to her bed in a dormitory without anything to eat or drink simply because she had become playful and talked during a meal. You were supposed to be silent and think only of God. Well, can you say you know a five-year-old child who is only thinking of God as she sits and eats her meager meal next to a friend? They will chatter away and forget they are not supposed to be talking. To them, God does not even enter into the picture.

Consequently, I was punished for being a child! Even in this day and age, parents forget a child is supposed to be free with joy, mischief, giggling, playfulness, and humor, difficult to control at times and certainly not constantly thinking of God.

The child may be dragged to church where she sits very bored and hears all of these explanations of what Heaven is like. The NOW is never mentioned; she has no concept of what Heaven is, for all she hears is what Hell is. However, since she does not believe in either one of them, she has to amuse herself. She looks around, moves her feet up and down because they do not reach the floor as she sits restlessly in the pew.

Church is finally over and she notes it is always on a Sunday. Her mind wonders, *why is it always on a Sunday? How come it cannot be on a Tuesday or a Thursday?* It then becomes a family ritual, and the family dynamics are played out. People refer to it as the custom to do this or the custom to do that. However, most families will not deviate from this ritual. The family might visit others; the family might have large dinners; or if the family is poor, it could sit for hours reading the Bible over its meager meal.

In my family during that time, there was a dinner prepared by the cooks and served to us by the servants. It was a restricted life. I was a child in that lifetime who had come to upset the apple cart—to not take on the restrictions; to display another way of interacting—another way of being. You have a saying that *that person is in the box.* Well I was definitely outside of the box, and I was punished for not playing the family game that was set before me.

As I matured, I set my own rules but they were rules I had made with great flexibility within them. At first they were rather comical, for when one is in the box, one must arise at a certain time. I made a point of either getting up at a later time, or an earlier time, as long as it was not the time that was designated for me to arise.

In the box, I was told what to wear. I made sure there was a little change in my costume. I would have different colored stockings; or I would put a different bow in my hair—just enough to be outside the box.

As I grew up, matured more, there came a time when my schooling was past, and my father talked about an arranged marriage. I put my foot down. Outside the box, there was no way I was going to marry that older, besotted gentleman, for he was a gentleman, all because he had position and money that my father wanted a piece of. It was like selling one's child to the highest bidder. Since I was a comely young girl, my father could ask a high price for me. And if an older gentleman was willing to sign the contract, the engagement would be announced.

However, I was not in agreement; there was no way that I was going to spend the rest of my years with that man who drank too much, had mistresses, and led a debauched type of life. I am smiling now for my way to avoid that, and there were not many choices during that time, was to tell my family I was going to join a religious order. I would become a nun; I would not marry. I did not care who it was; I was not going to marry. It was the only way I could avoid that fate of an arranged marriage. I found as time progressed that the choice actually was favorable to me.

I was able to start feeling the energies of God, my Father. The gifts that I had brought in with me started to flow through me, and I noticed that I was a healer. I could go into a sick room, put my hands on that brow just to feel the fever, so I thought, when lo and behold, the child would be up and running around the next day. I did not know what had happened. However, when these occurrences happened frequently, those around me started whispering, *she has the gift; she's a healer.*

Then I too started seeing a pattern; I could feel the energy running through me. It had a color to it; it was gold. I had never seen a gold streak before, except from the sun. I did not know what it meant. We did not have people who knew what it meant either, for each person had her own perception of what was going on.

I knew about Joan of Arc; I had read about her. I could commiserate with her. Yes, she had heard the voices, as she put it. She had seen the colors; she had known her purpose. I began to be led, to be guided. I would have an urge to go hither and yon. Then people started telling me there was a Light around me, and when I came into a room, it would light up. People would more or less automatically start lying down during the time I was there. I did not realize that it was a certain energy. These days, Fundamentalists call it *being slain by the spirit* where the preacher touches a person and he/she falls down.

I would enter a room and people would just kind of collapse, which I found rather upsetting for I did not know what was going on with them. I said to myself, *hmm, this must be something I am doing outside of the box*. I was very aware that I was unusual; that I was outside of the box!

I also was able to speak with God which I realize now was this telepathic communication. I was not aware of the terms to explain this in that lifetime. I just thought that everybody could hear this conversation in his or her head. I did not realize that that was unusual. I then would say to myself, *OK, you're outside the box once again.*

It became a way of life for me to live outside the box. I went where I was called, for I could feel people's energy beckoning me—calling to me. It was similar to my guides, my angels, taking me by the hand, leading me to some place and then finding out that the person had been mentally calling me. I would say to myself again, *hmm, I am outside that box.*

As I looked around the different places I went and interacted with humanity, I started making that distinction. *Oh, so this is what it is like in a box. There is no freedom—no freedom of thought. There is no peace.* There was a type of humor, but it was a humor that would be making fun of someone else. There would be no soft humor from the soul, which is part joyous at the same time. I could make these distinctions.

As I put my hands on the person who was mentally calling me—I don't know by what name, but I was known as the *Lady with the Light*—and as I laid my hands on them, it felt as if the angels just lifted my hands and placed them where the sickness was on that person. I did not do it consciously. The hands were just lifted and put down on the ill person. The heat would come. I could feel it come out my fingers. The person would feel peace; would feel love. Maybe it was the first time that that child felt love. It was not me healing the person; it was God's love taking away all the misery of their thoughts. It was more or less taking that person outside of the box where he/she could be in peace and love—where the child, the teenager, the adult could feel for the first time what it was like to be outside of the constrictions of the box.

I would be so filled with the Father's love; I would feel so much peace. I did not know that I was in the NOW energy. During those moments of healing those sick bodies, I was in the NOW; I was basking in that energy and those sick bodies drew it forth from me and merged with the energies that my hands were conveying to them.

Beloved readers, the NOW can never be approached when you are **in** the box. You need to let go of control; you need to let go of wants; you need to let go of anger; you need to be in your heart—the peace of your heart, the love of your inner heart—no ego; surrender, surrender into the NOW.

I bless you my beloveds. I AM known as your Mother Mary, but you can always reach me from that place in your heart. When you are in the NOW, ask for me from that place of NOW. Blessings.

(*And you, my child, are greatly loved; you do not always think about that. You are out of the box. Your abilities are out of the box. Take pleasure in that; know that you are doing what you are supposed to be doing; know that this is your purpose—to show people by example what being outside the box means; what being in the NOW means: peace, love, no control. I AM Mary, my beloved sister and daughter. Adieu.*)

Oh Jeshua, that was so powerful; she came into my heart so strongly; I feel tearful.

Dear one, as you write about the NOW, did you not think you would be experiencing it?

I never quite understood what the NOW was either.

So you see you were getting a taste of it also so you would know it; so you could carry that with you. Bask in this NOW; remain still for a while and be in the NOW, my beloved. We will resume our channeling on Thursday (30).

I bless you. I AM Jeshua ben Joseph.

(I sat in that loving energy for several minutes, not wanting to listen to the message on my answering machine, knowing it would dissipate the NOW energy if I did so; not yet able to sustain such pure, loving, and peaceful energy for any length of time.)

3

LORD OF JUSTICE

For this chapter, we will be bringing forth a Master whom you have not channeled before. I know that always makes you a little nervous, but we will let him introduce himself. Take a deep breath, and the next thought you will hear will be from this Master. (Do I call him Master, Lord, or what?) *He will give you his title.*

Good morning to this channel; I am so delighted and appreciative to be invited as part of your book. I am known as the *Lord of Justice* in my own right and on my own planet. I am from a planet that is an offshoot of Sirius.

We do not have the same vibration as those on Earth. We are human looking but we do not portray the human dynamics. We come from love, and one could say we are self-centered in the fact we are only love.

There is no war on our little planet. There is no jealousy; there is no covet-ness, where one person wants what the other has. We have none of that. We have the consciousness that is God the

Father's influence—His connection. We did not lose that as we came into our bodies.

We are human-like in the fact we do co-create in the manner that you do here on Earth. The mothers give birth as you do here also. However, the mothers give birth with joy; they give birth quickly and there is rarely any pain. If there is a tinge of discomfort, it would be similar to your body feeling a tug—a twinge in a muscle when you do your exercises. You would say, *oh, I have pulled a muscle*. It would be that type of pain, and it does not last.

All of our babies' births are successful. We do not have what you call *C-sections*, where you cut the mother's stomach area open so the baby can be pulled out. It is not necessary, for all of the births are natural, healthy, and appropriate. I say appropriate because the size of our babies is different from yours on Earth. We are a small race in stature, so our babies are small. They are healthy babies but only weigh in around 3-4 pounds. Rarely do we have babies that weigh as heavy as 6 pounds.

The mothers' range of height is approximately four feet, and we do not have any tall basketball players (*smile*). The male bodies are a little bit taller, but not by much. If we were in your jungles, we might be called *pigmies*. But we have a consciousness far above those natives.

We live pretty much in the NOW. This book is about describing what the NOW is. Would it be incredulous to think that there could be a whole planet that is just in the NOW—no fighting, no bickering, just peace and love? We are very industrious. We have fine minds. We can calculate quickly in our minds. Our children are educated almost from the time they can walk, which is rapidly attained.

We progress at a fast pace once we are born. Education is happening on a regular basis for it comes from the parents. All parents are teachers. They are not given the ability to co-create a child until they have reached the maturity of the mind in order to be able to teach what you would call philosophy, quantum physics, and the higher mathematical equations.

There are also great astronomers as well as astrologers on our planet. We are very much interested how the other star systems influence each other. There are billions of star systems and planets in the many, many Universes.

Technically, we have spaceships. Earth is still struggling because of fear to allow spaceships, extraterrestrial machines, to land in their space or be in their air space. On our planet, there is no fear; what is there to fear? Again, it is because of the maturity of our people. You may ask *is there any crime at all on your planet*? And we say NO, there is no crime because of the maturity of the people and the fact that they cannot co-create until they have reached maturity, until they have reached the facility of their mind to be teachers.

It is a built-in biological system—simply built in that a male cannot spread his seed until he is able to teach whom he creates what he will be producing! It is a very fine notion; is it not? *Yes, very interesting.*

Let us see what else we have. We have airplanes, but I suppose you would call them spaceships—flying ships that take off and arrive at their destination just a few minutes later. We use spaceships like you use airplanes. We have spaceships of course that can fly to outer space. The construction of those ships would be more endurable and be able to make those long distance journeys easily.

We navigate by the stars, and we send the ships out wherever we wish to go by thought. We do not need fuel or anything like that—just a thought and the ships take off. Many of the Lightworkers have spoken with the Commander Ashtar and the Admiral Sananda who have described the Mother ships. They are tremendous. One can be 1500 miles across so when you approach it, you think you are coming to a country. But you are merely approaching another ship. That concept is extremely difficult for people of Earth to take in. It does not make sense to them.

We have great minds in that we do have our philosophers. Our teachers write, and we have a library so that the child can read books of the planets and/or star seed's history. We do not have literature that is not true. You have literature that you call *fairy tales* or *fiction* and we do not have any of those categories. Everything one reads is the Truth.

Our philosophy says, why fill someone's head with false information? Why not have it be the Truth? We believe that is how on Earth the lies begin, for at such an early age children are told lies. They see the lies; your movies are full of lies. We have none of that. We have programs for the arts but they are live; they are people who represent someone—a great teacher if that is what the play is about. But again, it would be Truth that the people are seeing.

We do not have what you call *cinema* because again, many times there is little Truth and the stories are outrageous. They are sexually orientated and are meant to arouse people's passions. In our sphere, the people have passion, but it is a passion for learning, for knowing more of God the Father. We know of your Biblical stories; we know of your Jesus and all the characters of your Bible. However, we do not have that religion. One could say that we have no religion. We have in our minds just Truth. Our continence is a deep feeling of God, of the power of what is known as the NOW.

When you are living that and are feeling that, you do not need a false religion telling you another theory—how to practice another theory. If something like that started on our planet, it would cause discord and chaos. As you look at your Earth's religious history, look at all of the religions. Look at how people are still fighting and killing each other because that particular sect thinks it has more Truth than the other one—and it definitely does not. Therefore, we have no religions on our planet. This will probably shock many of you.

One of the things I wanted to address was the relationship between a man and a woman. We treat the opposite sex, whether a man or woman, with total respect. I have observed on your planet that males and females rarely respect each other. There is always an ego-ic battle for one-upmanship—for one to be dominating over the other. We do not have that dynamic. We have total equality.

We have a blending of the masculine and feminine energies so that when a man and woman come together with intent to be partners and co-create children, they blend so that there becomes a melding of the masculine and feminine energies. In your bodies, you carry the two energies. But on our planet, we are one or the other, and it is the joining that creates the two principles. When we are not joined in a relationship, then we are either masculine or we are either feminine. The goals of people on our planet are to be joined and rarely are we a people who do not have a mate. The relationships are shared in that children are shared with other members of a group that we are in, or the township, or the school, if there is one. Not every place has a school, nor does everyone go to school.

However, even the children respect each other. They can play and laugh joyfully as they try little tricks on each other. It is never with harm, but to give the tricked person a chance to problem solve. *How are you going to get out of this predicament?* It is all in fun, for we carry much humor on our planet; we are always in joy and fun.

You, channel, are writing a book on the NOW. And I come forward to give you a new perspective on what it is to be in the NOW constantly. People do not know any other way of being unless they have traveled to other worlds. We all believe in the Creator; we all believe in equality; we all believe in freedom— freedom of thought. We all believe in peace and we all believe in the deepest love that we can feel.

How many of you on Earth can say that? You have news reports all the time telling about who has killed whom; what horrible accident has occurred; what Mother Nature has done now—tornadoes, hurricanes, floods, fires, volcanoes, and earthquakes. We do not have that.

Someone from Earth might exclaim, *oh that is boring*! But when you are born into this type of living and consciousness, you know no other way of being. Therefore, you are not bored. You have your parents, children, fellow friends.

I have yet to talk about what we eat. We grow our own foods. We do not have dairy products for we have no such animals, nor would we eat them. We have no ice cream either. We are vegetarians. We have seeds we put into the ground, and they sprout and flourish into different types of leafy vegetables. You would call some types *lettuce*. We have tubular vegetables, but different from what you are used to. Our vegetables are very full of the nutrients that our bodies need. Our bodies need less of the proteins that you are used to getting from meats. We do not even use that term—*proteins*. We have nutrients that nourish our bodies.

We do not have set times in which to eat—breakfast, lunch, and dinner. We do not have that programming. We eat when we are hungry. It is not unusual to see someone eating in the late nighttime hours, early morning, or mid-afternoon. Anytime our body is hungry, we eat—six or eight times per day, if we wish to. Our young people do eat more often, for their digestive systems are not as mature or as large as an adult's.

Our foods do not need to be cooked, so we simply go to our gardens and harvest what we wish to eat. If they are a little dusty, we wash them off and eat the vegetables on the spot. We do have fruit trees, but our fruits are entirely different from anything you have seen or tasted.

We do not have insects that eat our food sources—our fruit. Your Plato wrote about his idea of a Utopia where everything was perfect. He was actually writing about the NOW but did not call it that.

This NOW is in our eco-systems so we have no harmful insects. We have beautiful fairies, you might call them—little insects with beautiful wings. Maybe you call them *butterflies* in many colors. We have birds in many colors also that flock together.

However, none of the insects or birds is ever eaten—nor predatory or dangerous to us. They are beautiful and when it is their time to what you would term *die,* they simply fade away, disintegrate, and disappear. They have gone into another dimension and back to Source.

We do not have any predatory animals. We have what you might call the cat family, but it is different in that they give you the love and purring, but they are not predatory. They do not kill the birds and eat them; they eat vegetables just like we do. There is no death, per se. They are similar to the birds in that they simply go into another dimension and go back to Source.

Our planet truly is a Utopia; there is no discord, no evil, and no black despair—only love, peace and living in the NOW. When the Father made that energy band so that the souls could come and be rejuvenated and bask in the energy, what you call the NOW, he also made a planet then that would carry that energy so that a whole civilization could be NOW energy. This is somewhat out of the reality that you experience on your planet.

I thank you for the privilege of speaking with you. I came through the portal that was open to me, and I will return the same way. I came by my own ship and shall leave by my own ship. Commander Ashtar was speaking of a large gathering, and I am part of that gathering. It is always good to travel so that one can see what it is like in other planets and star systems and know that you are not alone, that the Father has a myriad of planets with different ideas, different civilizations, different ways of being.

I leave you now. Again I thank you. I AM the Lord of Justice.

All right dear one; he is an off-planet Master of high degree. He touched on many things; much food for thought, shall we say. While this race is short in stature, they have brilliant minds.

Until tomorrow, my beloved, I bless you. I am Jeshua ben Joseph.

4

ARCHANGEL MICHAEL

Hello to this channel; how is my angel on Earth today? *Oh, you must be Archangel Michael!* Yes, I have the next chapter, and I am delighted. Let us begin. **I AM Archangel Michael**. My angels and I are always in the NOW. That is where we operate. That is where Truth is; that is where peace and love are, and it is an energy that is just a part of us—the NOW energy. We are not pulled to go back into that band of NOW energy as a *weary traveler,* for we came from other bands of energy. Our particular system does not require that energy. We just are. You have been told that the NOW energy is action with no action. That is what we are about. We wheel our action in a different way and we just are.

I wish to give you a story, for that seems to help you beloved readers to have another perspective, perhaps. This story is about someone—and you know I have helped millions and millions, so it is difficult to give a name to this person—but it is a true story.

This person was a young man; he was from this planet Earth, but in his upbringing, he was not given any of the spiritual tools that so many of you have and use. He was only fed the erroneous stories of the different religions. He was fed the Fundamentalist' outlook on things. His parents were strict, with his father being the dominant patriarch in the family.

He grew up in an atmosphere of discord because the doctrines that were fed him were not true, and he was brow beaten into learning those teachings. They were being programmed into him even though he fought against them mentally, for there was a part of him that knew the doctrines were not Truth.

And yet, how can a youth, for he was not a man yet, rebel against such a strong system? If he dared to take that step, he would be punished, which could be very severe. You have read about a schoolchild's knuckles being rapped severely with a ruler or a stick or a switch, for it was that era of history. Many times, he would come home from school with his hands bleeding.

His mother had more compassion, and she would clean and wash his hands, put a little cream on them and bandage them. However, she would tell him *now you know that you needed to have listened; you know that you did not do right*. Therefore, in a sense, she too was carrying on the discord, the lies—but at least she was doing it with an element of compassion and not agreeing with the degree of punishment her son was receiving.

As he matured, his path was laid out for him. He was to be a preacher like his father. He was to have a large congregation, one that would tithe generously, that would fill the offering-plates to overflowing as they were passed throughout the church. People were led to believe they were giving back to God freely. There was no such thing as giving freely. They gave because it was expected of them. This congregation was more well to do than other churches. Consequently, the offering plates were full when they were taken back to the accounting office. That was the expectation for him.

The young man felt despair; he felt hopeless, as though God had abandoned him. He wandered down to a babbling brook after services and knew that God was in the brook and in the birds chirping and flying around, but in some ways he could not feel Him.

He stared down at his feet and with a twig played with a pebble. When he looked up, there was a man sitting across the stream. The man also had a stick playing with a pebble. The boy-child yelled across *I did not see you come. How long have you been there?* The man replied, *oh, just for a while. I came because I could feel that you were dejected; you were in despair.* The boy was astonished. *You could feel me?* The man answered, *yes, I felt your unshed tears. I felt your unhappiness; I felt your loss of hope, so I wanted to come to you—to speak with you and to help you in ways you is not aware of.*

Therefore, the two male figures started up this conversation across the babbling brook. Neither stood up nor tried to get to the other side. They just talked loudly back and forth. It was safer not to get too close, and the male child knew he could just get up and run away if he felt threatened in any way. So they talked back and forth.

The child then started hearing musical chords. He looked around and did not see anything, but as he cocked his head, he realized the musical sound was coming from the babbling brook. He yelled across to the older man, *are you hearing that sound? It sounds as if the brook is playing music as it flows over the rocks.* The man replied, *oh yes, that is true; you are hearing Truth, you see. Always believe what your body is telling you, for that is Truth.*

They started discussing then what was true and what was not true. The boy would tell the man the different things he was taught in school that led to his bruised knuckles. The man across the brook would reply, *but you knew that was not Truth; you felt it; your body was telling you.* They talked and they talked until the boy realized that the sun was starting to set. He exclaimed, *oh, I've got to get home; I'll get punished if I am not there in time for dinner.* The man answered, *oh, all right. May I walk with you a while?* The boy agreed. *Yes, you can walk along with me; maybe you can come to dinner.* The man replied, *we shall see.*

They walked to the child's house. When they got there, they washed their hands at the faucet that was set up for that purpose, wiped their feet, paying attention to all of the rules, and entered the house. The child excitedly introduced the man to his parents and exclaimed, *this is a friendly man who was talking to me by the brook. So I invited him to come with me to the house; can he stay to dinner?* There was always an abundance of food in the house so the mother agreed while the father grumbled.

They sat and the father took out the family Bible getting ready to read his usual passages. Then the visitor spoke up and said, *may I say the prayer?* The father was somewhat startled but said, *yes, by all means.* The visitor then prayed, *I ask that the Father bless this family, that the angels come and speak with this boy and tell him Truth for he has not been hearing it! Guide him for he needs guidance. He has not been told his purpose, the way he is to go; guide him. I ask this in the Father's name, Amen.* Now the parent looked at this man. He had not pontificated with any verses and yet the simplicity of his prayer carried much love that the parent could feel. It puzzled him.

They ate their supper and the visitor chatted on about Nature, the trees and the birds and the babbling brook. Soon it was dark and the visitor rose, thanked the family and said it was time for him to leave. And he walked out the door, but he left behind a flower that had not been there before. The boy quickly got up, ran to the door and looked out, but the stranger had disappeared.

What they did not realize was that the visitor was one of my angels on assignment, bringing Truth into that house; bringing Truth that the young boy would feel and know and could trust and would prepare him for the work he was to do when he matured.

He grew into a much-loved preacher who spoke Truth and talked of the angels. He treated everyone kindly; he treated his own children kindly. He would not enroll them in school to be rapped on the knuckles. He home-schooled them and protected them from the ignorance of the so-called teachers.

Now that is my little story, but what was the purpose? What was the lesson in this story? It was to show you the difference when one is in the NOW and when one is not. When the child and the visitor were by the babbling brook, talking back and forth, they were in the NOW. When they arrived at the child's home, they had gone back into the energy of not having the NOW—the father getting into his rut of endless verbiage, most of which was not true. The angel, by saying a simple prayer, changed the dynamic and by the time he had left, the family was feeling the energy of NOW. NOW is action of no action; NOW is peace and love. NOW is camaraderie; NOW is Truth; NOW is contentment; NOW can have humor but with a sweetness to it—a love to it.

I bless you my dear one; we have been together for aeons of time. I have watched over you; I have guided you and I have loved you. At times, I know you felt that my love was lacking for you, but it was always there. I have severed cords for you; I have transmuted energies that no longer serve you by your request.

I AM Archangel Michael, keeper of the Excalibur sword, the blue sword of Truth, slicing away people's fears and discords. I carry peace; I carry love; I carry the NOW. I AM Michael.

All right, dear one, that was our Michael who is always with you. Until we meet again tomorrow (6-01-13), I AM Jeshua, with love.

5

THE TIBETAN DJWHAL KHUL

Hello, my dear channel; we have not spoken for many years. **I AM Djwhal Khul**. *Oh, Djwhal Khul, I have been thinking about you. We used to do my books in the very beginning, years ago (Books 1-2-3 & 5).* Yes, I thought it was about time I came back and gave you a little bit more information. This is information you will not find in *my* previous books written by the Tibetan (the Alice Bailey books), because I did not speak of the NOW in those books. However, the time has come where humanity needs to become more aware of this energy, for it is the goal of all souls to be in that NOW energy—the energy that is so complete, all consuming with love and peace. This is where souls are reluctant to leave and must have a little string of consciousness energy outside of the NOW in order to be pulled back out to begin work once again. Otherwise, it would just spend eternity basking in the Father's energy, and thus not getting any of His work done, nor evolving to higher consciousness.

You have transitioned brilliantly through the different dimensions. As you know, we call them *Initiations* in the Tibetan books, but they are really just progressions from one dimension to another. I know you wish for a level of anonymity, so I will not say what dimension you are at, but I know and you know it is very high and closer to the dimensions where the Masters sojourn.

I wish to tell you a story also. It seems to be the theme of this book—to use little vignettes to describe the NOW. These stories depict what the NOW energy would feel like. It is so simple, but it is a concept that people garble, making it more complicated than it is. Their mind gets into it, and they start making their own interpretations. *Oh, this is what they must mean; this is what happens.* However, most likely, those are conjectures on their part and it is not Truth at all. So let us begin my story.

Since I am known as *The Tibetan*, I have created a story that really happened, for we create our own reality, do we not? My story takes place in Tibet, before the Chinese came in and took over that land. I will narrate in first person, in order to make it more personal.

I was a little boy and (I have written this in one of our previous books.) I was out shepherding our long—haired goats. I heard this voice that told me to go to the temple and find my teacher. The story I wish to tell about the NOW is about what happened when I was in the temple.

There would be long hours of prayer and meditation, for the monks had what an outsider would call a *difficult life.* But for the monks, it was a *way of life*—a privilege to live in this austere way for God, to gain purity of thought. Since I was a Tibetan, my training needed to be for that type of body. I could not at that age go, say, to London and be trained by an Englishman. I had to be trained by a fellow Tibetan because that is what my body would resonate to. (We need to pick teachers who our bodies can resonate to. It has nothing to do with racism or anything of that nature, but simply the elementals in one's body must be compatible with the elementals in the other body that is teaching us.) Therefore, I was in the Tibetan temple being taught by the temple monks.

They taught in an amazing way; they taught by example. At first, you think that nothing is happening and the teacher is just sitting in contemplation and prayer. It seems to you that the monk is not paying that much attention to you. Therefore, as a child, you look around; you shift your position and try to get comfortable. You do not understand what is going on, for you are used to having people talk to you, instruct you, order you around and expect you to do this and to expect you to do that. Yet at the temple, you just sit there with what you think is no direction, no action. Does that not remind you of the NOW—action without action? That is how we were taught at the temple. We were taught action with no action.

We did not realize that our teacher, although he had his eyes closed, could see us very clearly through his spiritual eyesight. He studied our energies. He made little adjustments, with permission from our Higher Self. We as the students would feel a little tug here and there, like a sore muscle, and we would just go along with what we were being told to do.

If we stood up, we heard a very firm *ahem*. We looked around, and there did not seem to be anyone else except our teacher who appeared so deep in his prayer that we did not think it was he who had spoken. But the authority in the voice was enough to make us sit down again.

After what seemed like a long time and with my stomach just growling, which I am sure the teacher had heard by now, other monks came in with hot tea with goat butter melted in it. It was very nourishing and filled the void in our stomachs. I was not the only student in that class. There were five of us new converts going up that ladder to the Divine. We were restless. We played off each other's reactions all the time, not realizing that the teacher observed it all. This procedure went on for days and weeks at a time. We wondered when he was going to speak to us and teach us something. As far as we knew, no one had taught us anything yet. Little did we know at that time that we were being taught much— action with no action?

The monks were always in the NOW energy. We students popped in and out of it. If we could sit and go into deep meditation and join our teacher, we would be in the NOW. But most often, we sat with grainy knees, rumbling stomachs, childish squirming, but good intentions. These were all noted.

One day our teacher announced we were going on what you would call a *field trip*. We were going to take a hike. So we all stood up in single file and our teacher took us up this path. We climbed higher, and higher, and higher, to the point we were straggling while the teacher, as a robust hiker, climbed ever higher.

Finally, he stopped so we could catch up. When we did, we saw before us the whole vista of valley and surrounding mountains. It was very cold and we were shivering, but the teacher stood there as his warmth seemed to envelop him like a blanket. I am sure you have read that these great teachers had so much energy and heat that they melted the snow they stood on. As we glanced down at his feet, the snow had indeed melted. He was standing there in his warmth while we students shivered and stomped our feet on the mountainside. He knew that we were cold and hungry, so we did not tarry there long. When we started down, we children fairly flew down the trail, giggling, and pushing each other aside—typical young boys, vying for position. Finally, when we reached the temple again, we stood respectably aside so that our teacher could enter first. We boys then rushed in, shoving each other aside to see who could get into the warmth before the other. Ah, it felt so good to be warm again. The butter tea was immediately served and we sipped that with relish.

Later the teacher asked each of us individually while the other students listened, *what did you learn today? What did you see? What was the purpose of this trip? Do you wish to go again and if not, why not? What was it you had trouble with; what was it you did not like?* And so we told him about the cold, being hungry, the long hike, and yes, the vista was breath taking, but Master could we go back to the temple and get warm again?

No one mentioned the energy; no one mentioned the spiritual beauty of being there. The teacher just smiled and went on to the next student and the next. We five were in agreement. All we were feeling were the physical aspects of our trek. We thoroughly missed the object of our field trip (*chuckles*). The reason for going was over-ridden by our discomfort. We missed all of the spiritual aspects. We soon found out it was not going to be our one and only expedition, for it was going to be repeated many times. We would stand and appreciate the vista, but mentally we were so glad when the teacher led the way back to the temple and warmth with hot buttered tea awaiting us.

It got so we became used to the fact that we were going to go on the field trips. With all that exercise, we became athletically able to make the climb and sprint alongside our Master. This went on for several months until finally one of the students said, *Master, why do you take us to this same spot repeatedly? What is it you want us to learn?* "Ah," the Master said, "*you have finally recognized that there is a reason for these trips. That these are lessons in themselves.*"

With that revelation, other students started questioning. *What was the purpose? Why did you take us there? We were so cold. What was it you wanted us to learn? I saw this and I felt this.* The Master just listened and smiled. Then he started describing an energy to us. He did not call it the *NOW*; he just said it was an energy band that he wanted us to enter. He started showing us the energy that we were putting out and the energy that he was emitting during his prayer time and most all the other times including the times we made the trek.

Finally, it started to sink in. We were able to distinguish the difference in the energies. We were able to see where some of us were just practicing chaos. Others had just been more or less day dreaming, doing what kids do. Finally, it dawned on us that the lesson the teacher was giving us was profound in itself. We might have known that nothing that he did was unproductive. Everything had been thought out; everything had a purpose and a reason for being.

In this story, I will say we were being taught the energy of the *NOW*. It took us a while, but we did learn it. We did recognize when we were not maintaining that, when we had left the sanctity of that energy. We were told of the significance of it; that it was energy in our Father's House. Where could we experience that more but on top of a mountain, where everything was free of clutter and chaos? There was only the majesty of the vista before us. It took us a while but we finally understood.

Once we had gained that level of consciousness, we were able to reach new heights, to move upward, to be able to experience what the Master was telling us—to be able to digest his teachings.

Therefore, beloved readers, know that even when a story is as simple as this, that when each Master has come forward for this book, he has done so with the sole purpose of awakening within you the forgotten memory of the Father's energy of the NOW— peace, love, action with no action.

I thank you for the privilege of being here and telling my story.

I AM known as The Tibetan, Djwhal Khul.

Thank you, Djwhal Khul, that was great. It has been a long time, beloved, since you and I have gathered to put words into a book. It was good to be with you. *Thank you, Master. It was good to feel you also.*

(All right, dear one, that was our friend Djwhal, with an interesting little story that was different, but profound.)

6

LADY NADA

Hello, my dear one, **I AM** known as **Lady Nada**. And of course you know me, for I have come to you many times throughout the years.

I feel as though I am on assignment to bring you information on what it is like to be in the NOW—to help people recognize the NOW energy, to be able to say to themselves *oops, I am not in the NOW*. They can make the change and then carry the NOW consciousness with them wherever they are.

This is a little aside here, but your experience of being so totally lost yesterday brought home to you the emotional dynamic that many go through. One could be lost not only in directions, but lost in spiritual work, lost in soul work, lost in finding one's purpose. There are many ways of being lost, and when these souls are lost, they do have an emotional imbalance to them and literally feel that there is no goal.

To get back to today's talk; it seems as if the theme is for each Presenter to come up with a little story that would emphasize what it is like to either be in the NOW or out of it. Therefore, I too shall tell you a story. As you know, the stories are real, whether they happened to us or happened to someone we know. These are real stories, whereas we have said humanity feeds its children stories that are not true. Consequently, they hear fairy tales, or fantasies. Therefore, we wish to bring forth stories that are true so that no matter who reads them, they will know Truth when it is spoken. The following story did not happen to me, but it happened to someone who I recognized as a soul who had a true story. Therefore, with that soul's permission, I am telling it.

This story takes place on the spiritual levels. All of the other stories you have heard so far took place on the physical plane. I thought it would be of interest to you readers to know what it is like to be lost on the spiritual plane. You have heard that term the *lost soul,* and indeed, this story tells what that is like.

This channel had an experience yesterday in that she had an hour's drive in front of her in order to go to a family gathering. However, a section of the freeway she was on was closed that Sunday. She does not have a GPS in her car, and she was in the wrong lane in order to make the correct change, so she had to follow the flow of the lane, which led her in the opposite direction, backtracking where she had just been. Attempting to find the correct route to the gathering, she made many incorrect detours on unfamiliar streets. This took her out of the NOW, as she became more frustrated and emotionally drained with the problem solving.

Consequently, she experienced many of the dynamics that can happen to people when they become *lost* in whatever mode they are in—whether they are in the physical plane taking a college exam, whether they are in a spiritual group, whether they are on a freeway. The feeling of being lost is emotional, physical, exhausting, and not of the NOW. (However, the channel did find her way to the family party with the help of a kind stranger on one of the side streets who guided her as to what streets to take that would lead her back on the freeway and eventually to her family.)

This soul I am telling you about reached a point in her development, her advancement, where she literally became lost, not knowing how to proceed, not knowing what direction to take, not listening to guidance, being so wrapped up in the outcome that she kept going astray. Of course, she learned a great deal, for everything is a learning experience, no matter how uncomfortable it may be at the time.

Thereby, this dear soul was floundering, and she did not know what to do. When you are on the spiritual planes, there are rest areas where you can go. You can think of them as *rest stops,* if you wish. She went to one of those areas and she watched as other souls came to the rest stop, debilitated, out of energy, out of sorts, lost. They seemed to go on their way, either in the same condition or they found some help from the angels who are always there to lend a helping hand.

This soul noticed another woman who seemed friendly, so she went to her and exclaimed, *I just feel so lost. Do you ever feel that way? And the stranger replied, "On occasions, I have felt like that."* And they talked back and forth. Soon our lost soul started to feel lighter, as if something were being lifted off her. She exclaimed to the stranger, *what is it you have been doing with me? I know there* was *some type of energy that you were helping me with.* It was explained to her that indeed she was experiencing energy called the *NOW.* It was full of love and allowed you to just *be,* for the energy of NOW is action with no action. It just is.

The lost soul just felt this, and she started recognizing what it was like to be in your Father's House with NOW energy—this wonderful, loving, peaceful energy. It seemed to wipe away any perplexity, any tension she was feeling. After a while, she thanked the stranger and she went on her way, feeling lighter in her being.

You may be wondering, beloved readers, what is that dynamic that is in the NOW energy that has such a physical impact on a body, as well as a positive emotional impact on a soul, as well as a spiritual healing for the soul. What energy can do so much with so little effort? That explains the NOW. So much is done with such little effort.

When people first hear of the NOW energy, it is similar to hearing about a concept that may not interest you. Since you do not know anything about it, you are not interested in finding out either. There is just no interest until you become imbalanced in some way. Something has triggered you; you are not happy; you are not productive; you are not in sync with your life. What has happened? You have stepped out of any NOW energy you may have been in.

This energy is so potent; it has so many qualities to it. It is multi-dimensional. It just flows like a healing river through you. You can be in the NOW energy during sleep. You can set your intention so that in the morning when you awake *I wish to be in the NOW energy throughout the day.* When you meditate, you are in the NOW energy.

People think that when we go to church, the energy must be in the NOW. That is not correct. If people are very intuitive, as many of the parishioners are, they know when something feels off. Sitting in the pews, they are feeling uncomfortable because they have picked up the back room squabbles with a political air between the minister and the various people who run the church.

When the preacher goes to the pulpit, he carries that discordant energy with him while he makes all the ritual signs for peace and love on the cross. In the meantime, he is still inwardly in turmoil with his consciousness still back in the offices, for he has not finished his fight with the people who run the church. I do not believe that most parishioners realize the in-house bickering discord that goes on in a church.

A few years ago, this channel was looking for a church she could go to where she would feel the Father's and Jesus' energies. She sat through the sermon, came out and knew she would never enter that church again. She murmured to herself, *God and Jesus do not live here; they do not live in that church.*

In her own home, she has two huge paintings by Glenda Green. One depicts Jesus as a young man holding a lamb and the other one is of Sananda as a mature man. She has the one with the lamb hanging on the wall over her bed. (This bedroom is where she channels her books, also.) The Sananda painting hangs over her desk in the living room and is the first thing you see as you enter her home. She says many times to people, *Jesus lives in this house.* And that is true. His energy is throughout the house, as are many of the other Masters: Saint Germain, AA Michael, Mother Mary, God the Father (*chuckles*). She could hold her own church. After her experience in seeking other churches, she finally decided that the energy she was seeking was actually in her own home! So why not just stay home? As shocking as it may be to people, she does not go to church. Church is within her heart; church is in her house; church is in her books; church is right now as she channels this chapter, for she is in the NOW.

However, there are times she is not in the NOW—like yesterday when she got so lost on the way to her family gathering—for she is in a human body. That is human nature, so she did not beat herself up for it.

Here is a thought, beloveds. When someone berates him/herself, is that not ego in evidence? Is that not ego on a rampage? The NOW has no ego. If you are in the NOW energy, your ego is not forefront. You are operating from the God energy, the spiritual energies of the NOW.

Beloved ones, I have spoken on different ways in my little segment here of how to look at the NOW. Pick a mode of being that you are familiar with and say to yourself, *I carry one of those dynamics. This I can change. I can set my intent to be in the NOW. I will set my intent to change, to transmute the energies that were causing me discord. I will remember when I am berating myself, when I am angry at myself, when I am in ego and I have left the NOW. So I set my intent to acknowledge: "thank you, ego, for giving me this lesson; thank you, body, for this experience."*

You then have transmuted the energy and you have set the intent to be in peace and love. I do not believe that people are aware that by just setting the intent, they can change the energy. This channel makes a conscious intent when she has been emotionally impacted by family matters or with other issues. When she enters a room and she does not want to bring the energy of discord with her, she sets a conscious intent. She takes a few deep breaths: *Be in your heart; set your intent; be in the NOW.* She then enters the room.

It just becomes a way of life. Humanity needs to make some of these changes in its way of life—to appreciate the fact that the Father has given spiritual tools that one can use. All people have to do is set the intent and switch gears: *I am changing my energy to such and such,* and it will take you out of discord.

As I have noted, I have popped hither and yon. As I spoke, I would get an idea and then another idea would come to mind. This channel has so much going on in her life that she provides wonderful examples that she allows me to share (*chuckles*). I do get her permission, even though she is not always conscious of it (*more chuckles*).

Beloved readers, pick a mode of being that is yours and set the intention to change any of the discord that is within you. You will then be in the NOW and feel peace, love, and action with no action.

I bless you, beloved readers; you are moving forever upward and onward, as many of you say. It is a delight for us in the spiritual realms to see you.

I bless you; I AM known as Lady Nada, adieu.

All right, dear one, that is my better half, as we sometimes call her (smile). We will meet on Thursday (6-06-13). Much love to you, I AM Jeshua ben Joseph.*

---

* *Lady Nada is Lord Sananda's twin flame.*

7

MASTER JONAS

Hello dear, you and I have not met in this way before, but we have known each other from other worlds. Suffice to say that **I AM Master Jonas**. I come from a planet that is off-world. I came through the portal that was available on May 25, 2013. I come every once in a while to Earth to see how it is progressing. I say this not with pride and what you call ego, but the planet I come from is far more advanced than this great Being is. This Earth Being carries so much love and has many creations: all the fauna, the flora, the animals. It is stupendous what she has brought forth.

Our planet is mountainous also. We have great areas of lakes and oceans. However, the color of our waters is not of greens and blues but more of the purple hues. Everything on our planet is in shades of lavender.

We have a sun, of course. We have an education system; we have many features that you have on Earth, but in a more advanced stage.

Our stature is very tall. You could compare us to heights of your buildings. We adults grow from 30 to 35 feet; our young average around 15 feet. I know it seems incredulous, for we are extremely tall by your standards. Our bodies are similar in build to yours; therefore, our heads are massive and hold a large brain. While you use around 10-15% of your brain capacity, we use almost 90% of our brain's capacity.

We have brilliant mathematicians. We enjoy long debates as philosophers. We debate at deep levels the various wisdoms from the Father—All That Is.

Our children are playful but serious, in that there is no frivolity. It does not enter into their mind to be frivolous. They just are operating at an advanced mental state. There is joy and humor, of course, but all of higher vibration and dimensions.

We have pets similar to your cat family that are quite large, but in keeping in size for us. Everything on our planet is enlarged in order to be compatible with our statures.

We do not have houses, per se, but use the caverns inside of our mountains. Our mountains are quite beautiful. Their insides are full of crystals. The caverns are so gigantic, according to your standards, that we make them into rooms.

We live as a community. Thereby, there would not be just a few people living in one room, but a whole community sharing the various tasks—harvesting and preparing the meals and so forth. We do not cook our foods; we are vegetarians. There are berries, fruits, and edible vegetation in abundance above ground. We have no starvation on our planet.

We live many years, so we do not have old people dying on their feet or in wheelchairs with children caring for them. We live many hundreds of years, and when we feel our energy depleting, we have a celebration and a farewell party. We gather and talk to the one who is transitioning—parent, friend, a member of the community. We give gratitude to the person departing from us, thanking him/her for the friendship and service. The person then does not lie down, but simply fades away—disappears. The person has stepped into another dimension and is visible no more, having gone back to the Father. I know this sounds somewhat farfetched, but in your Bible, stories are written about the giants. There has been a time when some of our people visited your planet as giants.

Our mode of transportation is different from yours. Since our stature is so large, we do not have these super large machines to transport us. We move by thought. Everything is by vibration and dimension. There are areas where we can go and with the thought, just appear where we wish to be. We travel to many lands throughout our planet because it is so simple to get there.

We have libraries that the children are required to visit. There is a time allotted for each child who is to go to the library and read the material that tells of the history of our world and the other worlds around us. The history is not printed in books, for any size of a book would have to be tremendous in order to be held by these large hands.

Therefore, we have computers where the information is stored. I admit they are gigantic. The person sits in front of the computer and reads what is said but also just watches, for it is all moving— similar to your moving pictures. All information is registered on the computers. Nothing is lost; so the history is intact and, as I have said, can be viewed from one generation to the next. One can pick the different time levels that one wishes to visit.

When you go to your motion pictures, you may go to a show that is all about pioneer days, the war with your Indians, the covered wagons, the *Westerns*, you call them. You have pictures of violence, cops and robbers. We do not have that on our planet. Our nature carries no violence; we are not a violent people. Everything is there for us. All we need to do is to know how to harvest it. Our parents and teachers show us how to do this.

Therefore, if everything is provided for you, there is no need to grab someone's money, shall we say; or to steal from someone. It is not necessary. It is our nature that it is all there and always replenished. There is no want. If a person is hungry, the person goes to an area where the food is and just helps him/herself. Or if there is someone who is portioning out the food, one just asks for a portion.

We do have large appetites, for large bodies need much food. However, our kinds of food are so plentiful that there never is a lack. We have abundant light and sun; we have rain clouds. We have everything that is needed for vegetation to grow.

While we use the inside of mountains to be our living quarters, it is not because we dread the animals on the outside. It is because the inside of mountains is there for us; it provides shelter from the rain. Why not be comfortable away from the rain, so we go into the caverns. People may sleep outside if they wish. Some do. Some like to make long treks through areas they may not know about. They can lie down and rest when they wish.

We do not require long periods of sleep, such as your bodies do. We take what you would call *catnaps*. We may rest, lie down, doze for a couple of hours, and then we are good to go for a few more hours. It is built into our system where we run a high frequency; so we are always full of energy that stimulates us. We have a similar biological clock like you do within us, so that we can eat when we wish; sleep when we wish. Our bodies tell us. Our children tend to be more active so they do not have long sleep periods either.

We have no party system—politics. We have leaders, but they are learned positions. They are passed down from generation to generation. The Beings are very intelligent and very conscious, as well as being very fair. In your system, your politicians vie for supremacy; vie for a better position than another politician. We do not do that. We are all equal, even our leaders we view as being equal to everyone else.

Each soul has a purpose. If that purpose is to be a leader, that is what it is. It is what it is. We have people who enjoy working with their hands. We do not demean them in any way and think of them as beneath us. Everyone has a purpose and if that is what you were born into, it is what it is. Those workers are also very intelligent and vibrate on a very high level. The consciousness of the people on our planet is very high and they have brilliant minds.

You readers might be wondering if we have any type of punishment system like Earth does with trials and death penalties, jails and so forth. No, we do not. We have no death. As I have said as one's energy starts to deplete, that becomes a sign that it is time to make a transition. You just start to melt from view. You say your goodbyes and just disappear.

There are no weapons of mass destruction. They are not needed, if that is what you were thinking. We have no police system. We are self-governed—each person polices himself. We just know when one is in one's heart. There is no need to kill your neighbor. Why? We would not know how to do that anyway. Since we just disappear into another dimension, I suppose one could try to shove another into disappearing, but we do not know how to do that. Therefore, we are not a warring planet. We are peaceful and we are loving. And, we are huge, live underground but walk upon our planet. There is much love. There is co-creation.

When we want children, we just think about it. *Let's have a child between us.* We think what we want for that child and it soon appears. That is what I mean by co-creation. There is no penetration by the man into the woman's body. We do not co-create in those ways, for our bodies are not set up like that. We co-create by thought and plan what we would like our child to look like. When our planning is complete, we sit and the child appears. The child is usually one of our former relatives waiting to be re-born. When the child comes forth, he or she remembers. We do not have that veil of forgetfulness like you do. We remember.

I cannot think of anything else that would be of interest to speak about to you. Therefore, I will step back now and let your Master Jeshua come forward.

Thank you, Master Jonas. It was very interesting. You are welcome, dear soul; you have a deep heart. And you have yet to reach your stride in what you are doing on Earth. You touch the hearts of many people here and beyond but you are not aware of what you do. On our planet, we are aware of what we are doing in all dimensions.

I thank you for the opportunity to present my civilization to you. I have enjoyed our time together immensely.

Thank you, Master Jonas. I bid you goodbye for now. *Thank you.*

All right, dear one, that was different. Yes, you are coming up with different ones, that's for sure (*chuckles*).

8

MASTER SERAPIS BEY

Precious channel, **I AM** known as **Serapis Bey**. *Ah, hello.* It has been a long time since I last spoke with you, and it is a delight for me to be here doing so and to talk about this energy of the NOW. People wish to complicate it—to make it sound very studious and something to be studied. Whereas if they would just relax, be in their heart, and feel the peace, they would already be in the NOW and not even realize it. This energy is already on the planet.

The Father gave the NOW to people of Earth to use, for the energy has always existed. It was created when the Father started creating Beings, knowing there would come a time when the Beings would need to be rejuvenated and pulled back into His Source. Therefore, the energy is comparable to air. It just is; you breathe it; you live it, and you are it.

I come from arid deserts where it is difficult to maintain an aura of peace and stay in the heart. One's energy can become more lethargic because of the heat. The caravans would rest at an oasis and people would doze and not necessarily be in the NOW, but give themselves an adjustment because of the extreme heat. But during that time, they could be thinking of warring neighbors— nomads who might wish to come and steal from them.

You see, the mind plays a great part in being in the NOW. I say that because you do not want the mind playing a part. You want to be in the heart. If you are in the heart, you need not think how to best your neighbor. You think only of love and joyful things. I will give you a story that perhaps will bring you more clarity on NOW energy. Of course, this is a true story that happened to a fellow traveler a long time ago.

This was a young man who was very quick and had a good mind, but his heart was not deep. He did what was expected of him. He followed the right path but was ambitious. You have a saying where one climbs the back of another in order to get to where one wants to go. He would do that without a second thought, for his nature was a warring type of inheritance.

Every time that his caravan reached an oasis, while others dozed or slept away the hot periods of the day, he would scheme to get what he wanted. He did not realize that his scheming would be his downfall. One evening after the supper hour while the women were cleaning up and the men were sitting and having their after meal smoke, this young man went to the water hole.

As he sat by the edge of the water and trailed his fingers in the water, he saw in the water someone else looking up at him. He froze and his hand stealthfully went to his dagger, for if you are looking in the water and you see someone else, that person has to be standing behind you looking down on you also. Isn't that true? So he very carefully looked around and found that he was still alone. This astonished him.

He looked back down into the water and the face was still there looking up at him. Again he looked around, over his head, in back of him, and to the sides. He saw that everyone was still in his or her tent, and he could not fathom where the face was coming from. His mind started telling him that there must be a demon in that water. *I have to kill it or it is going to kill me!* So he took his dagger and kept stabbing at the face in the water—stabbing repeatedly. Every time the water settled down and cleared, the face would reappear, as if he had never disturbed the water. He did not know what to do. He did not want to cry out to the people in the tents for that would make him look like a coward in their eyes— that he could not take care of himself. He was a warrior, was he not?

After a while, he found himself calming down and he started wondering what was going on. He stared at the apparition and found that he was being drawn into the water. It felt as though he were going down, down, under and yet there was a part of him that still sat by the water's edge. He was drawn down close to the face.

He discovered it was the face of a beautiful woman, the loveliest woman he had ever seen. He could feel the love emanating from her heart. He put his hand out in order to draw her to him, but he could never quite reach her. There was always a distance no matter how hard he tried. She always remained not quite touchable. She smiled at him, and he could read her thoughts. Their thoughts went back and forth without either one uttering a word.

She asked about him. *Tell me about yourself; what do you think about; what are your goals; what do you do?* He would talk and talk to her until she smiled and disappeared. He then would find himself sitting by the water again. He stood up in kind of a daze, went back to his tent and just lay on the cushions through the night.

The next day when they traveled to another oasis, he found that his heart was thumping erratically. He felt drawn to go to the water to see if the apparition was in *this* water. Therefore, he could hardly wait until the sun set and they had had their dinner and everyone was free to smoke or to wander around. He hurried to the body of water and was pleased to find he would be alone.

He took a few deep breaths and peered into the water. There she was again. She greeted him, *come toward me; I wish to speak with you.* He felt himself falling into the water, and yet his body remained sitting at the water's edge. However, there was a part of him reaching toward the lovely woman once again. They talked for a long time, and he explained things that were in his heart that he had never spoken to anyone else about.

He spoke about his fears of growing into maturity and not being the leader—not being the man that he thought was expected of him. He admitted that he did not like the killing, the stealing, and the covet-ness of wanting something that was not his. They talked for many hours until once again, she disappeared and he went back to his tent, full of wonder.

This went on for several nights, with several stops at different oases. He was in a quandary. He did not know whom to talk to except for the lovely woman in the water. He made up his mind he was going to ask her for an explanation—what was the purpose of these watery visits, with his being drawn into the water and his trying to reach out to her, and their conversations night after night after night.

The next night the same thing happened; he was drawn into the water and felt himself floating toward the beautiful woman who held out her hand to him. He explained to her, *I cannot stand our meeting in the water night after night. And yet you do not let me touch you; you do not let me hold you; I am falling in love with you and you are driving me crazy!*

He spoke in the manner of a young man who is emboldened by love and brashly wants to conquer this lovely woman and make her his. And yet, she still held him at arm's length and encouraged him to talk about himself but not to touch her in any way. It was driving his senses to distraction; he was hot with frustration. He would stride back to his tent, throw himself upon his cushions, and lie there smoldering, half with anger and half with desire. And love was bursting in his heart. He had not felt this way ever, as far as he could remember. It was love; he knew it was love, but he did not know what he could do about it.

The next night when it happened once again, the woman came closer, the closest she had ever been. She touched his cheek and touched his heart and said, *what you are feeling is in your heart; you want me but I am you! I am in your heart; I have always been in your heart. I am love; I am the Divine; I am the woman that you want and I am telling you that she is already in your heart. Some day you will find her.*

Do not berate yourself; do not be angry, but stay in your heart and let this/our love grow, for you are not meant to kill and be a warrior. You are meant to love and lead. I bid you farewell. I will not show myself again; I will not come this watery way again, for I am in your heart now.

When you feel your heart, you will know that I am there; I am with you. You will meet the love of your life; you will meet me in the body of the woman you are meant to be with. You will honor her; you will love her with dignity and you will share your life with her and have many children. We are meant to be together. Do not grieve me; I am in your heart, so wait patiently for me to appear. With that message, she disappeared once again.

The man, half elated and half in sorrow, jumped with joy and ran to his tent and threw himself upon the cushions. He thought about her; he thought of her constantly. All the time, his heart was opening more and more. He was getting ready for the love of his life.

A week or so later, as they came to a different oasis, they found another caravan had just arrived also. He then saw the most beautiful woman he had ever seen. They made contact with their eyes, for she was covered with veils. However, her eyes spoke to him. He noted her tent and went there as tradition dictated, and spoke to her father, asking for her hand in marriage.

After much bickering, bargaining, and the signing of the contracts, he was able to have this beautiful woman as his bride. There was a great celebration a few weeks later as they became man and wife. His heart opened and he felt such joy. He could not even remember the man he had been—the man so full of pride and ego with a desire to kill so that he could be a man who demanded respect. He no longer had that desire; he only wanted peace and to bask in the love of his new wife.

To fast forward this story, they did have many children and lived into their old age, loving each other as they had done when they had first met in the waters.

This story may seem like a fairytale and in some ways, it is, but it is a tale of a man whose heart opened and was able to change from being one who only wanted to take a life to being one who gave life with love and peace. This story is the NOW energy. This story tells what the future generations can be like, although it may take 100 years or so. It will happen. Wars will stop and love will blossom.

I thank you for the privilege of speaking with you for this book. You are a dear soul, my child, and you carry the wisdom and the love that you have developed. You carry it forth and spread that energy in your books. You are greatly appreciated, and we love you.

I AM Serapis Bey.

Thank you Lord, thank you.

9

LADY KUAN YIN

Hello, my dearest one, **I AM Kuan Yin**. *Oh, Kuan Yin, it has been so long since I have talked with you.* Yes, it has, and I wanted to be part of this book. I have a story, as you can well imagine. I remember in one of your former books that I gave a story of how it was for a young girl to have her feet bound. Do you remember that? *Oh yes, I do.* Well I have another story, not mine, but a story of a friend who I knew. I will tell it in the third person.

There was a beautiful girl-child born into a peasant family. The family was hard working—the father and the mother both working in the rice fields, sorting, clearing, doing whatever was needed to keep the rice flourishing. The mother was heavy into her last month of pregnancy. When she felt the baby was to be born very soon, she lay down her hoe and went into their modest little home. She lay down on the blankets on the floor that served as her bed and gave birth to this precious little girl.

The little girl was a beauty from the very beginning. She showed no physical aspects of what one usually saw in peasants.

She had slim ankles, long tapered fingers, beautiful eyes, and as she matured, a tiny waist and long shiny black hair. She would have been what you called during your war times, a *pin-up* girl, for she was so beautiful. She was noticed in her village by the men and women who were jealous of her. She was different looking. One could not say she was a peasant, for she carried a light around her that belied that caste.

She soon caught the eye of wealthy men who were masterful and tyrants to the peasant villagers. The wealthy lived in large buildings and had many servants who were always beautifully attired and well mannered. They were taught from the beginning how to behave after these lords—not spiritual lords, but lords over you—had bought the beauties from their families and had them trained.

Therefore, our lovely little girl was sold to one of these lords of the village. The other women were jealous and the wealthy men were envious that this lord had acquired such a beauty. No one was allowed to touch her in a familiar way. She was going to be saved for the master of the house.

In the meantime, the child grew in maturity. Her beauty was known far and wide and she was very desirable. The men coveted her, for they liked and wanted something that they were not able to obtain.

Soon young men came to pay a call on this master, offering money to buy this woman as their wife. The master had bigger plans. He was looking toward her living in the palace with the Emperor and princes, so he held out for more money. When the princes in the palace started hearing about the beauty of this young woman, they came to call. They did not come to call like your southern gentlemen used to. They just rode their horses into the courtyard, threw the reins to the servants, strode into the house and demanded to see the girl.

When they saw her, she seemed to float silently into the room. She made a small bow with her eyes downcast. She held such dignity that the young princes bowed back and then became embarrassed, for their minds said, *she's nothing but a peasant!* But their eyes told them she was different—she was a princess, a goddess. She was from another world.

They bargained for her but nothing happened. The young princes pleaded to procure this young woman, but the master who owned her would not release his hold on her. He was waiting for what he called his *golden opportunity* when the highest official would want her and would pay an outstanding price for her. He had no idea that this beautiful girl-child had her own star that was leading her. She was well educated and had all the graces that a woman born into wealth and of a higher class held.

One day the master of the girl saw his opportunity. He was in the market place, and he saw a servant who belonged to a very high official. He talked to the official and got the information he wanted on how to present this beautiful woman to the high court in the palace. The official was impressed when he saw the young woman and also felt she would be a magnificent addition to the palace harem. Therefore, he told the village master how to connect and make arrangements to present the woman.

It was all done with cunning, contracts, changing monies from hand to hand to this official to that official until it had worked its way up to the top. The date was set where he was to bring forth the beauty he had kept under wraps. He dressed her as befitting a princess but was cunning in that he dressed her in a simple but elegant way, in white to show her purity and with some gold in her hair.

He instructed her to answer only questions from the high prince himself and to stay in a stately but respectful position—to bow low so she did not place herself higher than the prince—all the ways of being when one was in front of royalty.

Therefore, she was dressed and carried through the streets in a veiled chair, carried by four men who were also elegantly dressed. She was carried right into the receiving room and lowered to the floor. There was a hushed moment while people stopped talking and all stared at this curtained chair in order to see the beauty that was to appear.

The moment came. A servant lifted the curtains away from the chair and brought forth the beautiful young woman into the prince's presence. She had remembered her instructions well; so she floated to the prince and then bowed, waiting for the prince to raise her up. When he did, she lifted up her eyes and looked directly into his eyes. He felt a shock like a shock wave that went through him. He gasped; he could not believe it. She was a dream; he had never seen such beauty, such delicacy in human form. He knew he had to have her.

However, he was already married, so he made arrangements to have her taken into his harem where she was to reside for his pleasure. But interestingly enough, he was not able to touch this exquisite person. He was in such awe of her that he knew in some way that she must become his wife. She could not be just one of the women in his harem.

In those ancient times, he already had wives but they were numbered. As every new wife came into his life, the previous wife was lowered in position. She was no longer the number one wife.

Therefore, the bells rang and a great celebration occurred as the prince took this beautiful woman to be his number one wife. What he did not know was that this was destiny. This was their contract, the purpose of their souls to come together and to create exquisite children. This they did.

She helped the prince ban some of the senseless ways of having to act in the palace. She made adjustments and most of her ideas were accepted. She changed the energy of the palace just by her beauty, her peace, and her loving heart. She could walk into a room and the people would change. They might have been talking about a risqué story, but when she entered, the stories changed and became humorous and kind. All she did was to appear in the room.

Do you recognize that energy, dear readers—the NOW— action, walking into the room; no action, doing nothing but smiling and emanating love from her heart? She saw to it that her parents were well cared for, their life made easier—they were given extra food and comforts, not only for her parents, but also for the whole village, so that all felt her love.

This is a simple story, but it shows how when you carry the NOW energy, it changes the environment, it changes those around you. Remember action with no action, love and peace. It is easy, beloveds, to carry that energy, to be that energy and stay in Truth, for Truth will help you to connect to the NOW also. I AM Kuan Yin.

10

SAINT GERMAIN & PIERRE

Hello, my dear channel, **I AM Saint Germain**. *Oh, I love having you come, Saint Germain.* So we are back again, this time with a different story. I do like these little vignettes that speak Truth. So let us begin.

When I was in my youth, I had a friend. We were what one would call *close buddies*. And no, we were not gay, although royalty at that time had many who were gay. I must say I have had gay lives as part of mastering myself, but in this life, my friend and I were just straight guys. We were trying to learn about the world and ourselves.

This friend of mine, whom I shall name *Pierre*, was very ambitious. He was, in a way, not particularly wealthy, but he was comfortable. But he was determined to have more money. He could be called a *go-for*—go for this, go for that. He was willing to sell his time to any bidder who wanted something done. He was quite amenable in that he was flexible, so that if someone wanted something done that he himself did not want to do, he would contract with Pierre—no matter how small a request. Pierre would do it for a handsome tip. He was very honest and never cheated his many patrons. Therefore, he was called upon repeatedly.

It came to pass that he was called upon to be a liaison between two lovers. Pierre was just a young man in his teens and still not worldly, so he became intrigued with his new assignment. The gentleman who asked for Pierre's help wanted him to arrange an assignation with this beautiful woman who was under lock and key by her strict father. Therefore, he called upon Pierre to arrange a clever way so that the parents would be oblivious as to what was truly going to happen—the two soon-to-be-lovers could become more acquainted.

Therefore, Pierre would take on these types of contracts. *If you want to meet the love of your life, you must contact Pierre who has this innate ability to arrange such matters of the heart.* His reputation grew. The thankful Lords paid handsomely for such a service. They could not trust this request to just anybody because people were not honest back in that era. If people could cheat you, they would. If you let them cheat you, you were considered very naive or just plain stupid. But with Pierre, they knew it would be an honest day's work, and he would accomplish what he was asked to do.

Therefore, this became his livelihood—these liaisons between lovers. Now everything was going along splendidly until one day he was sent on a mission with a very large purse to purchase the affections of this beautiful lady. When I say purchase, I mean that Pierre would be paid and the lady would be contacted.

However, a glitch came up in this plan because, lo and behold, when Pierre set eyes on this woman for the first time, he was struck down in awe. He was in love! With the first glance, he was in love. He wanted this woman, and yet he had been paid handsomely to set up a meeting between this beauty and his latest patron.

Consequently, he moaned and groaned to me, *what shall I do? What do I do, Germain; what do I do?* I, of course, not having been in that position, could not really advise him. I could only be his friend and let him tell me his woes and to cry on my shoulder, so to speak.

It so happened the father, who was a nobleman, was looking for suitor for his daughter—one who would be suitable for her rank and station and preferably one who would be wealthy so that his daughter would have everything that she was raised to have. This would mean a beautiful place to live, opulent gowns, jewelry, and carriages. *How was all of this going to end*, bemoaned Pierre?

It is interesting as one advances in years to note how the Universe will step in and just solve the problems—bring a solution—if one will be patient enough to just listen and watch for a sign. Pierre was beside himself. He wanted the money he was paid for this liaison, but his heart reacted so to think about giving her up to another man.

Now in those days it did not mean all that much at first whether the woman gave her heart to the man or not, because everything was arranged. All the marriages were arranged because of the huge dowries that were involved. It was also advisable for the courting gentleman to have money. However, as history has proven, many a woman with a large dowry married a penniless nobleman simply so that she could have his title.

Now it so happened that my friend, Pierre, was in that last category. He had no stately funds, but he was a nobleman and he carried a title that would come to him when his father died, for he was the first-born son. Time marched on, and Pierre finally was forced to arrange the meeting his latest patron had contracted for.

In the meantime, Pierre's father was suddenly struck ill and died, leaving his title to his first son, my friend, and making him a great nobleman. He was not particularly a rich noble, but he had a title that would impress a wife and make her happy. Therefore, when Pierre called upon the beautiful woman's father to present his patron's proposition, the father asked Pierre about himself. *What about you, young sir? I hear you are now a great nobleman. Would you not like to have my daughter as your wife?* Of course, Pierre stuttered and admitted yes, he would, but he was kind of standing in line for her hand. It was his patron who was the first one asking for the marriage contract.

The father knew about the patron; he was an older man with tendencies to gamble. The father decided that his daughter would be happier with a younger man who not only had a title, but who also was honest. If his daughter's dowry was going to be squandered in any way, the father preferred that it would be Pierre who handled her money.

Interestingly enough, when the father rejected the patron's proposal and offered his daughter to Pierre, Pierre honestly told the father what had happened. By this time, the patron had his eye on another woman, and he really did not care that much—he was a gambler and it did not mean that much to him. Therefore, he released Pierre from that contract who then returned all the money he had been given to set up the liaison. As I have said, he was an honest man.

In that wonderful way that the Universe can provide, Pierre fell into his way of working for others, by being a *go-for*. By being flexible and allowing "come what come may," he was led to the love of his life. It led him in an honest way to this beautiful woman whose heart went out to him when she saw him. They had a lavish wedding that the father provided, and so Pierre was married to this beautiful woman. As the saying goes in fairy tales, *they lived happily ever after*.

These little vignettes in this book seem like little fairy tales—to read one per day, to read to one's children as a nighttime story, perhaps. Each one is so different and yet each one holds parts of the lesson of the NOW energy. Pierre was a do-er. He took action and then waited—no action while the Universe provided for him the love of his life.

Dear readers, allow yourself time to let the Divine Universe provide for you. Be patient, trust, and know that your Highest Soul is watching over you and will bring to you, when the timing is correct, what you are supposed to have, where you are supposed to be and will take care of you. The Universe will provide if you will but allow it in peace, love, and silence. You take the one step and then you wait and are still. Be still and trust; be in your heart—that is the NOW energy.*

I AM Saint Germain.

Oh thank you, Saint Germain, that was a wonderful story—a very nice lesson. Thank you. You are welcome.

Adieu.

---

* *Author: I often hum this old hymn: "Be still and know that I am your God; be still and know that I am your God; be still and know; be still and know; be still and know that I am your God." This reminds me of the NOW energy.*

11

LADY NADA—VISIONS

Good morning, dear one, **I AM Lady Nada** once again. *Hello, Lady Nada (chuckles).* I have come with a second vignette for your readers.

I had a friend who was very competitive. No matter what she did, she had to be sure that she was capable of doing her very best. She forgot at times that she was not carrying the whole team on her shoulders—that they were a team and everyone had a part to play. It was a shared responsibility. However, she found at times that she took it all upon herself, and she would cry and cry as her fear would rise up. She then was sure that her team would lose or something might happen and it would be her fault. Of course, that was just not true.

She was very good at what she did, but one day when she had played extra hard for the team, she fell. She twisted her ankle badly. It came very close to being broken, and it swelled so rapidly and so large that the medical team could not make that diagnosis at first. She was told to stay off that foot and not walk on it. She was in tears. She felt she had let the team down, and she took it all upon her shoulders. She sank into despair. She withdrew into herself and poured out her frustrations upon everyone who was around her.

She tried to think of other things to do, but she really could not think of anything she could do without using her foot. She did not want to sit and just look out the window. She did not want to sit in the serenity of Nature. All she could think about was *who was playing in the ball game in her absence!*

One day, as it so happened, she found herself alone. Her mother and father were out doing their projects. Her siblings were in school. There was a wrapped sandwich sitting on the table beside her for her lunch. She knew it was going to be a long day with nothing to do. She went into self-pity. Her pattern for releasing self-pity was to become angry. She became angry at her body, which caused her foot to ache more and more. The angrier she became, the more her foot hurt.

Her bedroom was upstairs and the only way she could escape her room was to slide along on her bottom out the door. She chose to do this and then thumped her way down the stairs and through the door that led to the swimming pool. She was able to raise herself up, unlock the latch and enter the pool area. She hopped onto a chair and sat dejectedly staring at the water.

It was a warm day, and she thought that maybe her foot would feel better in the cool water. Since no one was around, she took off most of her clothes, down to her undergarments. She then hopped over to the pool's edge and gratefully fell in. She tumbled to the bottom and then allowed her body to float gently up. She was a good swimmer since she perfected every sport she decided to play.

So she lay on her back in the water and just floated. She noticed that gradually the swelling of her foot was going down. She would say to herself, *thank gosh, my foot is not broken; thank gosh, my foot is starting to feel better.* Every time she made that statement, she was thanking the body-elementals for healing her foot, although she did not know this. After a while, she was able to hoist herself out of the pool and hop to a chair. She sprawled in the chair for a long time. She started to doze, and she thought she was dreaming, but she actually was having visions.

She saw herself when she was much younger and she would have these dramatic meltdowns. She noticed that every time she was angry, there was a part of her body that reacted to the anger. It would hurt; it would hurt until she released her anger in some way. The hurt would then go away.

The dream-vision then changed. She was older, and she saw herself playing with others. She saw how she reacted when she was not pleased—how she took her anger out upon others. She always reacted as the victim, never seeing her part in the play. But each time she experienced a short little vision, she found a piece of her personal puzzle. She started putting the pieces together.

She saw how she was hurting her body with her anger. She saw how she used her anger to get her way, to manipulate others. As she became older and played more on the sport-teams, she saw how she controlled people with her anger and made them do things her way—what she wanted. Then a part of her body would hurt.

With this last episode in one of her meltdowns, she noticed in her vision that it was the worst one yet and seemed to go right to her foot. That was when she fell. She realized that all the anger she was feeling was being carried by that foot—being carried forward so that she had that experience time after time. She started seeing this pattern in these visions. It was like watching a motion picture develop. She was feeling more dejected—more like a failure, not quite knowing how to correct it. She sat for a long time, remembering all the little visions that she had had. She knew they were about her going back to when she was a child up to now when she is in her teen years. She realized if she kept the way she was acting, she would have a rough time in her future.

She was being shown two paths to walk—one was the old way of reacting in anger with anything that displeased her, always someone else's fault, with no accountability. The other path was in lighter shades of color, and she saw that when she was in her heart and loving people, that if she did something that seemed to be a mistake, she could say *oops, I need to change that.* She then would change her attitude and her body would not hurt.

Consequently, she grew up to be a beautiful woman, lovely in every way. People would come to her, for she was wise. She had learned and she guided them and helped them see many of the ways that she previously had been. She grew to be a lovely woman, as I have said, and went on to have a very successful life.

The moral of this story, of course, was to show you what was *not* NOW energy. Manipulation, anger, no accountability is not NOW energy. And yet, it seems to be the energy that so many people carry today. It does not seem to matter whether they are young, middle aged, or older, if they have not grown and been guided to make a change in their life, they end up bitter, old people—cranky and difficult to be around. Their caretakers were always glad when they had finished their shift.

Those who choose another pathway choose to keep growing, to change their energies, to recognize where they could have done better with their lives—to excel, to follow their guidance, to hear their soul and to connect with it. They use the NOW energy to advance, for the NOW energy is the way Home—back to the Father, back to the Source.

Every person will come to that crossroads in his or her lifetime. If that person has been listening to the guidance of the angels and soul, the person would be well on his way, well on her way to higher advancement, to the Master that he/she is and may yet realize.

I give you this story, for parts of it are Truth and parts of it are yet to happen. It all depends on what the young person decides, does it not? There are two paths. Which one are you on? Make your choice, and if you need to change, my prayer for you is that you will do so with a full heart.

I AM known as Lady Nada. Adieu.

All right, dear one, that was another little vignette that could be anyone's child—anybody's granddaughter or grandson. Let us say it is a clear picture of humanity. What direction is it going; what path is it going to choose? Each person on the planet comes to that point on his/her journey where a decision will be made and changes will occur. Blessings to our readers,

I AM Jeshua ben Joseph, your brother.

12

FATHER-MOTHER GOD

Hello, My dear channel and to these dear readers. **I AM** known as your **Father/Mother God.** I so enjoy it when I can contribute a few words to these books, for you see, each word contains energy. The energy is uplifting. This book is about the NOW energy—what it means, what it is, and how to recognize it. I think after 11 chapters you have a fair idea of how to recognize it—to recognize when you are hearing it in others and when you are in it yourself.

You have been told that the NOW is heart; it is silence. You have a term called that *pregnant silence.* The NOW is action with no action, but with a most pregnant silence, waiting for you to tap into it; waiting for you to bask in its healing energies. If you can be in the NOW even for a few minutes each day, it will bring health and rejuvenation to your body. You see, when your body was created, it was created in the NOW energy. It knows that peace and love; it knows what it is like to be held in a loving embrace.

When souls are created, they are created, of course, with the Mother/Father's thoughts, for is not the Mother the nurturing one?

Is she not the Holy Spirit, although the Evangelical Christian still wishes to make her masculine? That is that ole-time-religion. That is that old way of being, patriarchal, where everything has to be masculine. Therefore, they take this most powerful energy, the Holy Spirit, and make it masculine, as they made Me. They saw God only as a masculine Being.

Is it too farfetched to think that when your Jesus/Yeshua walked the Earth, he was not allowed to have a woman to love, to be with him, to be his wife? And YES, to have children? The patriarchs would not give him this way of being, this privilege, for they thought that that was only for those who were the lesser Beings, the lesser gods. If you are going to have a God, He has to be above the lesser. There cannot be anything sexual about a God. The lesser gods, of course, can have all the sex they wish. And they do, but that is not for the man they made into a God.

My children, those are such erroneous beliefs given to you by the religions that are man-made, the religions foisted upon you—full of all of those lies. There is no Truth there. I have come here today to speak about some of this Truth because it is very much about the NOW energy. NOW energy is Truth. When one is in the NOW, one is also in Truth.

My beloved Holy Spirit and I created these souls, these *Monads*, as you call them. When you have a baby who comes from a great Being, is *it* not also considered a great Being? I am saying this without ego. Ego is such an earthbound way of reacting and thinking. In my world that I have created, there is no ego. There is only Truth and love.

I wish to comment further on the religions. Although this book has these little vignettes that mothers and fathers might read to their children, the adults may also enjoy these little stories of Truth. But, My dear readers, the energies need to change. Humanity needs to change. There are wars; different countries talk about needing nuclear weapons; chemicals are being fired upon the so-called *enemy*. For what? Because "*my* way is better than your way." Take my way or the highway—the highway away from Me—the the highway spelled low-way, the 101. If you do not agree with me—what is that saying, *get out of Dodge*. The Western movies have a specific way of speaking—*get out of Dodge City.*

I am digressing, but I have so much to say to you. I feel My heart full—full of love for you. Some day you will know that feeling. Did you know there is a depth—different depths—to your heart chakra? Did you know you could have a shallow heart—meaning it has no depth to it? That person cannot love any deeper. The wife feels unfulfilled and does not know why. She may start looking elsewhere for love that is deeper.

The same applies to men. If his wife is frivolous without a deep heart, he too will look with a wandering eye. You see, the NOW energy builds the depth of your heart. There is a sacred passage that you can go through to your sacred heart. You can enter from your back, between the shoulder blades. You can meditate from there. You grow the depth of your heart. As people grow this depth, they may have days when they are just crying and they do not understand why. It is because their heart is growing.

Your chakras grow and, since they are attached to different areas of your body, you may feel pressure in those areas. You may wonder what is wrong with your body. If you are looking through your third eye, which is between the eyebrows, at times it can feel like a headache. It might ache but it is only to alert you that you are expanding that chakra—the chakra is growing so that you can perceive more accurately and receive visions. This is all part of growing depth in chakras.

You have been told in our books that when your third chakra, which is around your belly, starts to grow, it protrudes outward. It pushes outward, so you are no longer taking in the energy around you. Masters do not take *in* the energies around them. All of you who are straining to master yourselves, your third chakra, your belly chakra, could be protruding outward. It is no longer concaved, but convexed, going outward.

When it is concaved, energies are coming into you. You become a sponge from the energies of everybody's chakras. However, when it protrudes, your chakras, your energy is going outward. It is similar to a beacon on a lighthouse. Yes, you have Light coming out of your crown chakra, but you also have Light coming out of your belly! Consequently, people feel this as they come toward you. NOW energy. You can recognize it. It is peaceful.

The energy coming out of your belly is a part of you—your peacefulness going toward others mixed with your large heart expanding outward and engulfing them. You become a walking magnet; people are drawn to you. It is your energy. They feel better after being in your presence.

Jesus did not have to do anything but walk among humanity, which he did. Of course, he was impacted also, for people not understanding how energies work would try to take that energy from him. They did not realize they could build it within themselves. One cannot take another's NOW energy. That becomes your personal signet.

Your personal signet has energy within energies, within energies, within energies. No one has the same; no one can take it from you unless you allow it. Your NOW energy becomes a personalized signet—like wearing a signet ring. In the olden times, the noblemen had signet rings. They pressed them into wax that sealed their messages. Anyone who received that message saw the wax signet; knew it was real and that it was an important document for him. The NOW energy becomes your personal signet.

Therefore, you see, dear readers, your NOW energy of *action* is the development of your chakras. The *no action* is the emanating of these beautiful energies, coming forth from your body, that influence everyone around you. True Masters have energies so wide spread that people could feel them coming, even though they could not yet see them.

I am so happy to be with you today, My children. I urge you to heed your hearts, to bask in the NOW energy. It takes no effort;

it is effortless. It is rejuvenating, but effortless. It permeates everything, but effortlessly. You see all the action it is, but with no action.

Children of My heart, I know your prayers; I know your sorrows. I know your joys and I wish you great joy in your endeavors. Always find joy in whatever you do that is from the heart—that is from the Light that you carry. Find your joy; be in the NOW.

I bless you, My children. I AM your Father/Mother God—All That Is.

Oh Father, thank you so much for the beautiful message and blessing. Thank you for that.

And you, My dear daughter, at times wear yourself out with your Virgo-ness. Just know you have yet to hit your stride. I think you have been told this already; you have yet to hit your stride. Your age-years have nothing to do with it. Your years stretch ahead of you as far as one can see. You have a young body and your strength and love are beautiful to behold. I love you, dear daughter; I love you.

Thank you, God.

Jesus: All right, dear one, how was that? *Oh wow, I was not expecting that. That was wonderful. He just covered so many topics. It makes me chuckle; it was fabulous. And He came on Father's Day!*

We will sit again in a couple of days and leave it at that. *Thank you, Jeshua.* Bless you, beloved; bless you.

13

DJWHAL KHUL—DEATH

Good morning, my precious channel. I AM the Master that has come to you many times before, a long time ago. **I AM** known as **The Tibetan, Djwhal Khul**. *Good morning, Djwhal Khul. Thank you for coming.*

We have another little vignette for you. This one reaches out more broadly and speaks about a more worldly subject. Remember from the Alice Bailey books that I was known as *The Tibetan*. In those circles of learning, I still am, but I have also branched out so that most know me as *Djwhal Khul*. There is still another group of people who have not heard about me at all. Be that as it may, it makes no difference to me. My ego is not involved.

We are going to speak about an interesting subject, an interesting one, for it involves everybody—your transition, your death. Now that brings fear into most people's hearts, for most are not ready to meet their Maker. As they have been told, *when you meet your Maker,* people say, *this will happen; when you meet your*

Maker, He will judge you. And most of the time the words you hear being preached are not correct.

You have been told that going through that door is a transition. You close the one behind you and open another door in front of you and walk through it. Yes, there are helping hands welcoming you and it is similar to attending a large party. There are people milling around. They could be past relatives or angels. They also could be future Beings who will be part of your next game plan. They mill around and speak softly. No one shouts; it is not necessary. They just commune in a soft way of speaking. No one has deaf ears—a hearing deficiency. Therefore, all words that are spoken are heard. The souls hearing the words hear them on several levels.

You have an astral body, and most of the souls are wearing their astral body for a while. Therefore, you hear with those ears. Your senses also pick up the words; remember your senses—the touch, the smell, the hearing. So you pick up what is said by the words that are spoken.

The energy is of the NOW energy. There is no rushing around; there is no particular *hostess with the most-est.* There are angels who greet you. Everyone greets you and is in joy—delighted to see you again. We will call one of the arrivals by a short name—Pete. *Hey Pete, long time, no see; how did it go for you?*

Pete is still in kind of a daze with his passing. He smiles; he is happy. Part of him has already forgotten how old he was, how ill his body was. He feels WONDERFUL! This channel's sister died of multiple sclerosis—the dreaded MS. At the end of her life, very few of her body parts were functioning. She could not walk; she could barely breathe. However, a few weeks after her death, she appeared in a dream to her sister, this channel, and exclaimed, *look, I can walk again!*

Here she was, looking like she did when around 30 years of age. She wore a white bathing suit, as she had when she lived in Hawaii. Her red hair was blowing in the breeze. And she was walking effortlessly! She seemed full of vitality and joy.

Dear readers, let go of your fear. There is nothing to be afraid of. You know, as youngsters go to school, they have so many dynamics bombarding them—their fears of riding the bus. Will they find a seat? Will the bullies attack them? There also are the dreaded stories of lunchtime. Would someone try to steal their lunch money? There are so many games that people play out on each other. Would anyone want to sit with them? Once the child is in his schoolroom, will the teacher call upon him? And, perhaps he would not know the answers.

Pete went through all of these fears. Every time there was a new situation, his body would panic. He would feel nauseated, short of breath. He put on a brave front and became too loud, too jovial, to cover up his lack of courage. He was so much in fear.

The child from the very early stages was programmed to be afraid of everything that was new. Do you not think just the term *death* would hold similar fears? The child from early childhood was so afraid that he carried that fear throughout his lifetime. He then passed his fears on to his children, for the great unknown was something to be feared.

Religions perpetuated fear as the preachers started bringing in the concept of a devil. *If you do not do this, the devil will get you. It is a sin to do that; you are going to go to Hell. Also, when you come to the right-hand side of God, boy, will He get you! You'll get yours!* All the erroneous messages you were given throughout your life bombard you. And you passed them on to others as well.

Consequently, why would you not be afraid of death? Wasn't that the ultimate fear? All those times you were afraid, was it not because you were afraid you were going to be killed in some horrible way? Therefore, would you not be afraid when you heard the doctor say you were dying? Or if you had been shot and knew you were going to die, would this not be fearsome for you?

So many lies—there is little Truth given you throughout your lifetime. Readers, let go of the lies; let go of the so-called facts, which are not facts, given to you by religious leaders, by your teachers, by your parents, and by your peers, for everyone has built upon his or her own programming of lies. Everyone is afraid; everyone is afraid to go through that door that is called *death*.

In my day as the Tibetan, we would say prayers, the body would die and then it was respectfully transported to an area where the buzzards would peck on it—peck it clean. Tibet is a land of rocks. There is no place to bury bodies in the ground. What did they then do with the dead bodies? They had the animals—the birds—peck them clean. The bones were then broken up and stored in different designated areas—similar to your cemeteries—except the areas were underground caverns for the storing of bones. The stacked bones carried a name. *These are the bones that belonged to Pete; these are the bones . . .* And so the stacks carried the name for generations.

Each culture has a different way of dealing with death. In the United States, the wealthy have gone too far the other way, in my opinion. There are these huge cemetery plots with elaborate statues, elaborate headstones. The body is put into a waterproofed coffin that costs many thousands of dollars and then lowered into a crypt that is also waterproofed—a cement cave, a cement coffin within a coffin. There is nothing about *ashes to ashes; dust to dust. Let the flesh go back to the Earth.* None of that is honored. Now in some cases, when the body is so full of cancer, it needs to be burned in order to release that energy, to transmute those cells that carry cancer.

Too many of these bodies are buried with their cancer still intact and it is now poisoning that plot of land. No wonder there are great earthquakes, great fires, great tsunamis, and great hurricanes in order to cleanse that land. In the Midwest and on the east coast of America where they recently have had such devastating tornadoes and savage storms, the earth was being churned up like a farmer spading dirt, or a plumber with a rotor-rooter burrowing down deep to release this energy that is full of disease from years back—years back! It is so impacted with disease and ill health. People wonder when they live in those places why there is such illness; why so many are dying. It is the energy that those plots of land still hold.

The Indians had it right when they did not want the white settlers building on their burial grounds. The Indians were keeping the land sacred, but also there was this deeper meaning: let the Earth breathe; let it release through the seasons, through the climate changes. But to build right on top of a burial plot or cemetery, you are just building on someone else's *sewer.* I know that sounds harsh, but that is Truth. You are building this beautiful house on someone else's plot of land that is now a sewer because of the diseased body(s).

People have so much to learn about death. They have so much to learn about energies—how they need to be broken up when they are clumped together, turning malevolent. That is why it can be so healing when one is near the oceans. The water has the ions that clean your energy. Ought one to live right at the water's edge? Not if the area is one of earthquakes; not if the land rests right on the tectonic plates that keep moving. The oceans are beautiful to see and feel, but they are not really safe to live by, for the hurricanes also will come. That is nature's way.

This little vignette is more of a teaching guide than a story. As children read this book, or as the parents read the book to the children, they will receive different ideas, different aspects of how to approach death. There is nothing to fear. You just go through a door; the veil is lifted and you have an entirely new perspective. You see things differently. You feel lighter and you get to greet those who have gone through the doorway before you.

Do not fear death, beloved readers. As Jeshua has taught us, lay your body down and leave it. Let the elements reclaim it; let the Earth reclaim it. I know it is not that easy anymore, but the teaching is still there. Do not be attached to your body. There are many elderly people who are very attached to their body. Their body can be totally deaf and blind, barely able to walk, be incontinent, and yet the soul does not want to detach from its body.

The soul is not in present time. The soul is not in the NOW energy. The soul is remembering how it used to be: *Oh, I remember when I had this body and it was so healthy, so pretty. I had all of these beautiful clothes; I did all of . . .* It forgets it is now almost in a vegetative state. It is causing great anguish throughout the family members. It is a burden to them. Yet the soul is oblivious to this. The soul wants to keep remembering its past. It wants to keep the body alive so it can remember the good old days when it was young and beautiful and not the wrinkled, degenerative one it is now.

Do not be attached to your bodies, dear readers. Let them go. This lifetime is but a blink of an eye to the soul, for old souls are millions of years old. Therefore, your lifetimes are just a blink and then the lifetime is over. Let them go. Do not be attached to them. You came in with your lessons; you know what they are, and you leave with those lessons, either finished or unfinished.

You can then look at them afterward. *Oh, that's why I did that.* Do not compromise the lesson you came to learn by refusing to leave—to detach—from your body. Do not put yourself in the position where you have to come back to your daughter in a dream and remorsefully say, *how can you ever forgive me? How can you ever forgive me for the anguish I put you through, for having to take care of my aged body, changing my diapers; how can you ever forgive me?*

Therefore, you see, dear friend, much happens when death comes, for that is the grand de-tachment. That is the grand escape and the grand beckoning to a wonderful new journey.

Peace be with you, dear readers, blessings, and may your journeys in the NOW energy be productive with no action.

I AM Djwhal Khul, The Tibetan. I bless you.

Oh, Djwhal Khul, that needed to be said, thank you.

Yes, dear one, it did need to be said. I AM Djwhal Khul, until we meet again.

14

DJWHAL KHUL—HEAVEN

Jeshua: Dear one, we are going to give you the title of this book, which will surprise you. We wish to call it: <u>NOW Energy for Now and Forever</u>. *And yes, the word Now is in there twice. It is not NOW for Eternity; it is NOW Energy for Now and Forever. The book is about half finished and many of the Masters who came in will return with other comments. You will see the book change just a bit in direction. This next Master is an encore Presenter, so I shall step aside and let him speak.*

Hello, dear one, you have had me before. Your mind is trying to unravel all the different Masters who have come before. I was just here and gave you the chapter on Death. *Oh, Djwhal Khul, you return!* Yes, for there was more that I wished to say on that subject. So this is chapter 14 and **I AM Djwhal Khul, The Tibetan**.

Up until now in this book, we various Masters have been giving little vignettes that were fine examples of what the NOW energy is and also what it is not. Saint Germain's vignette on the

Royals' gluttony is a great example of what the NOW energy is not.

The last time I spoke, readers, I spoke of death. That can be a heavy subject for many people. However, for those on the other side, they are quite pleased with their transitions, if all went smoothly. There has been so much talk about Heaven versus Hell. The emphasis today will be on that subject. Most of the Lightworkers agree that there is no Hell. Hell is of your choosing. Hell is a concept of the various religions that is not factual. Therefore, I will make the statement: *there is no Hell*. That is a fact. Some say *there is no Heaven*. We say that is in the eyes of the beholder, for there are astral planes that let those who have made their transition feel at home in all the splendor they did not have while in a body, perhaps. And all the love they did not have—all the opulence that they may not have had.

There is that fictitious picture of Heaven with Saint Peter standing at the *pearly gates*—huge gates made of pearls. The streets are paved in gold. If you arrive with that belief system that is what you will see.

Others who do not believe that will find a garden party going on. Still others may find they are in an infirmary recovering, for if they were extremely ill, their belief systems would say, *I need a doctor; or I need to be resuscitated; I need to be rejuvenated.* All of that is given to them because it is their belief system. And yes, a debilitated body is in need of care, but it is a care of love—to be totally loved. That heals the body, heals the mind, heals the heart.

Of course, visitors can come to the infirmary, similar to when a mother gives birth and all the relatives flock in to see the new baby. The same happens to people when they pass. The relatives come to see them. In the last chapter, we talked about *Pete*, remember? *Hey, Pete, how are you doing?* Therefore, you have all of your relatives giving you jovial greetings: *we're so glad to see you.* Later, those who had not treated the person very well when alive come forth and ask for forgiveness. Forgiveness is still very important to every soul, for it is a combination of Light and love and yes, the NOW energy.

People arrive at the gates, if you want to use that term, and they may carry so much guilt. They can also even have hatred in their heart. They hated their neighbor or hated someone at their work place. That is all ego. Ego is trying to be superior. Many people with self-worth issues need the ego versus connection to their soul to make them feel worthy, which would bring them love and great comfort. *Forgiveness* is very important, for you need to give, to give love. *Forgive*ness—*for*—you need to *give* of yourself.

In your world, you have gated communities, and there is a gate. Only those who live in the community can enter or leave. So you have a gated community in your imagination called *Heaven*. People wander around in the fineries they have always wanted—gorgeous furs, for example. Well, that is sort of a thing of the past because of the love for the animals. However, there are still those who covet a fur coat.

Consequently, you will see this as you walk the streets in Heaven—the fur coats. Others want the jewelry. You will see huge precious stones in necklaces, bracelets, and rings adorning the people.

Many people, like the men, had lost their hair and arrived bald. They want a head of hair. Therefore, you will see men walking around with great heads of hair. Before they passed, the women, of course, were conscious of their figures. Many exclaim, *everything on me has gone south!* You get the picture. Therefore, you will see women with beautiful figures on your walks around Heaven. You can walk through the woods, if that was what you loved during your past nature walks; or along the beach, if that was your dream; or along lakeshores. All of this is possible in Heaven—you are choosing each experience.

But, there are different levels. There are the healing levels, which I called the *infirmaries*. As you go further up the ladder in philosophy, you address the facts of your religious beliefs and many of your other beliefs. Many people arrive with what is known as *homophobia*. They are aghast to find out that they have had several lifetimes as a homosexual themselves. They understand now. Everyone has a lifetime(s) of a sexual preference being the dominate force in that lifetime.

Masters are *androgynous*. They carry both the masculine and feminine principles within themselves. They need to know what each of those principles means and feels like. You know Earth is a great schoolhouse, as you have been told. Therefore, the soul keeps sending its fingers of consciousness out to experience this.

As a male, you may wonder what's it like to have a baby growing inside of you. What is motherhood all about? Consequently, in another lifetime, guess what? You are a mother so you can experience that—experience your belly growing outward until the button protrudes. And, of course with that experience, it does not end until the actual birth with all the pain involved. It is an experience the souls wish to have, for they are developing themselves—reawakening much within themselves. Therefore, there are many aspects of one's journey in lifetimes that are addressed while in Heaven.

Masters can bypass this section of God's world if they wish, and they have the level of enlightenment to do so. There are all levels of Masters. Every attainment has levels to it. A good example of that would be your school systems. You go through grades one to twelve. Each grade is a learning experience with a learning curve of different levels. When you have achieved that, you can go off to college with different levels and then graduate school with more levels to achieve.

That is very similar to gaining your Master-hood—Masters *at* different levels. There is no judgment here. Again, let us use the example of your school systems. *Oh, that person is in the fourth grade; oh, that one is in tenth grade; that one is in college!* It just is. Masters have a choice. They can work more on Earth, or they can go to other worlds.

Let us speak of Joy. There are all levels of Joy. You are beginning to see that nothing is without these levels because they are multi-dimensional. The same holds true for the NOW energy. It is multi-dimensional.

We could use the example of your oceans, perhaps. You are wading in an ocean. You walk out and the water becomes deeper and deeper until you are forced to swim. Then the water deepens further, and you have to wear a diving suit if you swim into the depths, for the pressure is too great. You have to wear breathing equipment in order to get enough oxygen. The depths can be in miles; the colors change.

The Father does not create in a singular way. There are always dimensions and depth to anything that has been created. Look at your human body. Scientists are still trying to find out how the brain works, how the mind works, how Creation works —multi-dimensional.

When readers read a book, if they themselves are not consciously aware of their many dimensions, they will pick books or levels of entertainment that are just third dimensional in themselves. They go for what is called more or less the *Jack and Jill* books. Jack went to the market. Jill went to the fair. As the soul progresses, starts making different transitions, and reaches different dimensions, the soul's world expands. It sees many levels it was not able to see before. Consequently, one can see why the soul keeps returning to Earth for its many experiences. **The experiences are what give the soul its depth, its levels of mastery.**

I started off by speaking of Heaven and Hell. As I have said, there is no Hell. That is only in your distorted belief system. I say *distorted* because that belief comes from old-time-religion. If you expect to see a Hell and burn forever, you will find yourself going to such a place that you think would be a Hell—with the torture, the screaming, and the fires. Everything that you imagined Hell to be, you will find until you start moaning, *oh God, get me out of here; oh God . . .*

Soon you will see angels full of Light. Are you finished playing this game? Do you realize this is all illusionary? You still are not quite sure, but all you know is that you just want to get out of there. *I'll change; what do I have to do?* The angels then bring you to another aspect of being. You think, *oh, I want to go to Heaven.* So they will take you there, through the pearly gates so you can play out your game again—the furs, the jewels, the fancy cars, men with full heads of hair, women in perfect bodies. All of this will be played out. You will have your new houses. You will re-create in Heaven everything you did not have while in a body.

You may go to the infirmary first and spend time in the healing levels there. You also will have your life's review and view what you could have done differently—to see what life is all about. You will learn what it means to have different levels of enlightenment. You will then meet with a group of souls, set up your future game plan, come back to Earth, be born, and start it all over again.

Or, you can make a choice. You are no longer repeatedly going to be on that karmic wheel of reincarnation. Leave that belief system and make the choice to go off world, to see something new, to experience something new, to go to the NOW, to the Father and bask in that energy and its different levels.

The Father is always creating. The Father must keep bringing in new ideas also. And then you start to realize that not only do you have many souls, but also there are many Gods and many Universes, and you can make the choice as to what road you are going to travel. Do you travel the one most people take, or do you choose the one less traveled—choices, dear reader, always choices along the way.

I AM Djwhal Khul, The Tibetan.

15

KUAN YIN—POVERTY

Good morning, my dear channel, **I AM Lady Kuan Yin**. *Ah, hello, Kuan Yin.* What I love about these books is that we get to come back more than once to speak with you and to blend with your energy. I am most delighted. Before I start, dear one, I wish to say to you what a beautiful heart you have. Every time I come, it has grown deeper and broader and encompasses more than you have any idea.

When a Master goes forth, his heart reaches out to humanity, to animals, and to nature. Therefore, one at a Master level is always leading with his or her heart. That is what you do. I wanted to bring this to your attention so you would become more aware of the fact that when you enter a room, it is your heart energy that enters first. It is your heart that people feel and are drawn to. *Thank you, Kuan Yin.*

Now, we will not exactly give you a vignette, but we will do some teaching here for the readers of this book. I envision this book being read to children, to those not quite ready to read for themselves. Therefore, they start out young being told about the NOW energy. It is so important that the children have this foundation, for it will support their belief structure.

In previous times, so much of the old beliefs from the ole-time-religion got a finger-hold on a person. It then grew and grew and grew. Giving you these vignettes not only by me but also by the others starts this foundation. It gives people a finger-hold on Truth versus a religious dogmatic lie. The Truth is of NOW energy. This energy is so full of love and so non-judgmental. It just is.

People often wonder what does that mean when someone says, *it just is*? People have such a tendency to mold something that fits their beliefs; they want to mold it into something they have been taught. In that way they can understand it better. The NOW energy does not do that. It cannot mold someone. It just is. The person comes to it. You come to that energy by embracing it, by allowing it to be—energy you can sit in and know without effort that it is permeating your very soul, permeating all the cells in your body. It just is. It permeates and infuses the Light of the Father—the love. It also carries an element of *hope*.

When you are in NOW energy, there is hope within you that all is well, that you cannot be harmed. You are in the Father's energy, and no harm can come to you. Therefore, there is that element of *hope*.

When children grow up—meaning they are in their formative years—they carry a great deal of fear that they have picked up from their parents, from their teachers, from their church, from the religions, from peers. They just pick up humanity's fear. Hope is smothered when one is in fear. If a child can be taught early enough about the NOW energy—that it just is; that there is nothing to do but bask in it—his/her *hope* will flourish. The child will know what he is to accomplish, what he is to do in this lifetime. He or she just knows.

I had parents who were quite enlightened. They knew if they loved me and allowed me to be who I was, I would find my path.

They did not put any blocks in front of me. They watched over me to be sure I was not harmed, but basically, I was given free rein as to what I wished to do. Of course, since I am called the *Lady of Compassion*, I had much to learn. I had pain and grief in my life. My parents knew that was all part of my training, and they did not try to shield me from it, for this is what I sought to do. This was my soul's purpose, my soul's progress—to experience pain so that compassion could grow out of my wounded heart. This it did. It took several lifetimes. One does not gain this level of mastery in just one lifetime. I will say one usually does not. There is always an exception to any statement like that.

Consequently, I grew up in years emotionally. I sought areas of great poverty. I deliberately had gone there to see what that was all about. What would it be like to have such poverty? Would I be able to remain steadfast in my love for God? My parents had not taught me religion, per se, but they taught me the higher perspective, the higher levels of the Father and Mother.

Therefore, I went to a village where one could say it was in total poverty. Of course, back in that era years ago, there was no plumbing, no electricity, or anything of that nature. But just because one had to light a candle in order to have light or put a candle in a lantern in order to carry some light, that was not poverty. That was simply living in that time period where one had to be inventive to keep light in a room. You have heard that term, *I just went to bed with the chickens and got up when the rooster crowed.* It became a way of life. However, the poverty I am speaking of is when a family was all jammed into one room with no light. They did not have any money to buy candles, nor to buy the necessary wax in order to make a candle. If people cannot afford that type of light—a simple candle—then they are definitely below the poverty level.

The family was below the poverty level when it came to food. The children in the village were given assignments to go to other villages to see what food they could steal. You have seen movies, perhaps, where monkeys come and steal food—people had to remain vigilant and protect their food or the monkeys, those marauders, would come and steal all of it!

The wealthier villages became aware that if they did not protect their food, the children from the poorer villages would come and steal whatever was left unattended. You have in your folk tales stories of the mother or grandmother baking a pie and putting it on her windowsill to cool. Well, for one, the women in these villages did not bake pies, nor would they leave food on windowsills because of these marauding villagers—everyone scrambling for something to eat.

That was my assignment—to go to one of these villages and stay and become part of that community, to be able to use my wits to see how I was going to eat, and of course, to open my heart more so my compassion would evolve. If one is hungry enough, there becomes a fine line there between crying from the pain of hunger, which can lead to self-pity, versus crying because his or her neighbor is even worse off.

Mothers watched their children cry—their little stomachs were empty. It was painful for both of them. Mothers did everything they could to lessen that. They would find pebbles small enough to put into a small mouth, but large enough so that the baby could not swallow it. The child would suck on that stone, trying to chew it and yet not being able to. The relief was only mental. It did not go down as far as the empty stomach.

Since I was part of that community, I could not relieve their hunger, for I also was hungry. I searched the countryside for wild plants that I could eat or I could bring back to a family. I went forth and watched the animals. I saw the rabbits nibbling on a certain plant. So I nibbled on that plant and noted I did not become sick. Therefore, I knew I could harvest those plants and take them back to the villagers for them to eat. This I did.

I also watched the birds to see what they were eating. If you have watched a bird, you will note the bird will peck a piece of fruit and never eat the whole thing. I watched to see what the birds were eating. If they found a particular seed that they ate or a particular plant they pecked on, I would try eating that also, and then I took some back to the village. Of course, if there were any wild fruit, the villagers had long ago pillaged all of that.

So the question becomes was there NOW energy in that village? Or was there only self-pity, self-deprivation, self-anguish? Since I was part of that community, I felt my heart go out to them. But since I too was very hungry and felt the pain of it, I cannot say I was a great help to them. I held their babies and washed them and found pebbles for them to suck on. When I brought back some leaves that the bunnies had been chewing, I washed the leaves and pounded them with a rock so that the leaves became mushy and could be digested. It helped a bit; it helped me, for I ate them also. I carried a great deal of hope. I found myself searching, hoping I could find something to eat. I also went out from the village to hunt for food and leaves.

I am telling you this, readers, because while the NOW energy is available, people on an emotional level need to come to it, need to be in peace so that they can bask in that energy. However, if they are starving, the NOW energy seems to be unattainable. And yet, it is there. This is where people with a more advanced level of consciousness can emotionally reach for something to bring them solace.

Hunger is a great leveler for people. Ego does not have much of a chance to flourish in that environment. But the inner spirit is strong; survival is strong. Those villagers who were determined to survive did so. Of course, the lesson would be how did they do it? Yes, they may have taken someone else's food from a more prosperous village, but did they actually harm someone? Did they kill for it? That is the big lesson. Will you step over that boundary and kill for that piece of bread? Those with an enlightenment that was trying to shine through did not kill, but they themselves might have died from starvation.

It seems so harsh, but souls wanted that experience. They wanted to know—*can I withstand this and keep my ideals alive, keep my soul untarnished?* It was a most difficult lesson, but it grew *compassion*. Poverty is a great teacher, for it grows your compassion; it grows the development of the heart, and it will lead you to the NOW energy. Remember it is action with no action. By searching for food in the forest, watching the animals, one could be in the NOW energy, waiting for a sign from the animals to show the way, to show where the food is.

I bless you, dear readers. I come to you today to show you how compassion can be grown and flourish and how it can lead you to the NOW energy.

I AM Kuan Yin. *Thank you, Kuan Yin, for the amazing story.*

All right, dear one, that was Kuan Yin on poverty, *a sober story, is it not? And yet, humanity all over the globe has experienced this and many are still experiencing this—the pangs of hunger.*

Until next time, I AM Jeshua ben Joseph.

16

LORD SERAPIS BEY—LEADER

Ah, beloved one, it is so good to be back. **I AM Serapis Bey.** *Oh, hello, Lord.* I have told you in a previous chapter about a young man seeing his reflection in the water hole. It brought back some more memories.

There were always warring factions among the various nomad tribes. You see, they were a warring people, descendants of warriors. It was in the blood; it was genetic. Therefore, they were always ready for a fight, always suspicious of anyone they did not know. It was important to them to strike first, so that they would not be killed.

The children were raised that way. A young boy would be given his first knife. The knife was not as large and dangerous as his father's, for the scabbard was smaller so that the youth's knife would fit in. However, he could and did use it. He played with it; he practiced with it; he learned with it. He got so that he would kill small animals with it just to know what it was like to kill.

At times, his father would go off with other warriors to participate in a skirmish, and when the warriors came back, there would be many tales of heroism. *This one is a hero; he did this. This one is a coward; he fled the scene, but we rode him down and killed him.* It was said with such pride. The boys then would be proud of their fathers for having killed the so-called enemy.

As one particular boy matured, a strange thing happened to him. He was not that delighted having to kill something. He noticed that he admired a beautiful animal. He laughed at the little animals that popped their heads up out of their holes. He loved the animals and if he did not need to, he did not kill them. If he had to kill animals in order to prove his prowess among his peers, he did so with a heavy heart. He did not know what to do, for this was a new experience for him. He did not know what was going on with him.

In every tribe, there was a wise man. The wise man usually was not a warrior. He had risen above that. He guided the tribe. He may guide them to war on another tribe, but he himself did not participate.

These tribes had their particular gods that they bowed to, that they prayed to. Some would say it could be Mohammed or Allah. So there was a remnant of spirituality. Therefore, when this man-child came to the priest of the tribe, the youth sat there respectably, waiting for the priest to acknowledge him. The priest had his eyes closed while he observed the student.

He saw a young man full of ideals. He saw a heart that was fluttering, trying to break through the confines, the belief systems, to kill. He saw a great spirituality ready to blossom forth from this young adult. He saw the struggle within the man, for these belief systems had been passed down to him. His own heart, his own spirituality had started to question these.

He did not want to kill. The struggle was *if I do not kill, I will be labeled a coward.* He knew he was not a coward, but at the same time, there was the ego within him. He wanted to prove he was not a coward, but he did not want to kill in order to prove it. Consequently, he had this inner war going on in his heart. The priest, who was a conscious one, who was a man of his god, a man of enlightenment, saw all of this in the young man.

He questioned the lad, delving into his beliefs, seeing how far the boy had gotten in his struggle against the usual way of being for a young man in this tribe. He talked to him and told him to come to him every day and just sit. He did not have to talk or say anything. He was just to come and sit.

When the lad sat with the priest, he was told to take his scabbard off and to lay it to one side, as it was not needed. Therefore, every day for many days the youth came, took his scabbard off, laid it aside and sat with this Master. Soon the youth started having these different concepts, these different ideas that would just come into his mind. He started to question: *why was there killing; why did people kill each other when no one had done anything to them?*

The priest started asking the lad what his thoughts were. They exchanged ideas back and forth. The boy then was allowed to release these negative beliefs, and the Truth that the priest spoke started to permeate the lad's heart. As the days and weeks progressed, his heart grew until he felt he no longer could aspire to be a warrior. He felt he was being called to be a spiritual leader in some way. Then he doubted that and felt that was grandiose thinking. *I am just a peasant.* But the priest assured him that it was their god's way of naming him as the priest's successor. The priest was older in body and knew his time was drawing near when he would lay that body down and go on to other things—spiritual things.

Therefore, he started grooming the lad, telling him he would be his successor and be the leader of that tribe. He was not to be afraid; he was to know that he had been chosen; this was his destiny. Since these nomads believed in destinies, the lad accepted the responsibility that it was his destiny to be the successor of the priest.

When the priest laid his body down and died, the tribe turned to the young man, for it had been proclaimed that he was to be the new spiritual leader. At the time the tribe turned its focus on the young man and accepted him as their spiritual leader, he laid his scabbard down and then stood with his arms outstretched and his head looking up toward the Heavens.

All the tribe saw this Light ascend on him. This Light was so bright that the tribe fell to its knees, for this was the sign that this young man was the chosen one for their tribe. The tribe believed in spiritual signs; they were superstitious. All signs pointed to this young man. He was their spiritual leader; he was chosen by their god.

The story I have told you is true. This was not the only story of this kind, for all the nomads, all the tribes had a spiritual leader. These leaders were not chosen by the ego but by a spiritual sign from above. The tribe then just knew they were being shown a new leader to love and to respect and to know that Truth would always be spoken from him.

This little story is one of NOW energy. It shows how, as one's heart changes from being a warrior to being one of peace, the NOW energy grows until one is in this energy, of this energy. There is no effort. The lad made no effort to be in the NOW; as his heart changed, the energy around him changed also. He was greatly respected and lived to his old age—having spotted *his* protégé, having taught the lad what he would need to know and how to be a spiritual leader.

This is true for anyone. You may not be a great spiritual leader of hundreds of people, but you can be a leader of your own soul. You can stand in Light and love and be deeply connected with your soul and with God.

I AM the Lord Serapis Bey, and I greet you this day. *Thank you, Lord.* You are welcome, my child—and you are one of those leaders, one of those silent watchers and leaders. I bless you, my child. *Thank you, Lord.*

17

MASTER JONAS—WANDERER

Hello, dear one, I know in America this is your 4ᵗʰ of July, the time for celebration for your Independence. Keep in mind it is not only independence for your country, but it is independence for yourself—independence from co-dependency from family. Independence, dear one, is very important at this time for humanity's steps up that ladder, for that evolution; we Masters are never dependent upon someone else. We carry our independence within us. We can love and have relationships, but we are always independent; so happy 4ᵗʰ of July; happy Independence Day, beloved, and the same to these readers.

Good morning, channel and to the readers. **I AM** known as the **Lord Master Jonas**. I came in to present before. Since this is your Independence Day, I wanted to bring to you a true story about our independence. As I have said in my pervious chapter, we are a very tall people. We are the giants that walked your Earth. We were not the Red giants, for they were a different people, but we too walked the Earth.

It may seem astonishing to you but we were not dependent on each other. We were a world within ourselves. Even the young people, the youngsters, once they were weaned from their mother's breast, became independent. The more they matured and were able to walk and talk clearly through all of those stages of development, the more independent they became. There would be times when the child would take off investigating his or her whereabouts—exploring his little world. How far did it go? Of course, there was no fear from the mother. She knew the child had just gone to investigate and that he would find his way back.

The child read the signs; he followed the shadows. When the shadow was at a certain spot, he knew that was a signpost. If he were gone any length of time, he would wait for that shadow to appear again. No one was lost on our planet. They knew where they were going and what they were seeking and what was needed. There was no fear; they knew they were safe.

Now you may chalk that up to the fact that they were so tall they did not need to fear other people. However, other people did not come to our planet. There were so many worlds to discover that we did not have these visitors from which you would call *off-world*. We were somewhat isolated, and therefore, we could keep our independence. There was no one coming to try to control us—to capture us.

We had great resources of value but the space marauders did not know this, so we were safe in our own little world. However, once in a while, one of the youths would attempt to explore before he was really physically and emotionally able to do this. He just took off by himself and he saw things he was not prepared to see. He saw different animals that looked ferocious but were actually somewhat tame as they came and sniffed him. He was not yet full height so that the animals could be larger than he was.

However, one particular youth was so inquisitive, even more so than most of his peers, that he approached the animals without fear. The animals sensed that lack of fear. He had not come to threaten them, to kill them for their pelts and then eat them. He did not carry that thought within him.

As you are learning, readers, each world has its own god. We have a god that you would pray to. We did not think of it as *praying*. We merely thought of it as talking to an ancestor. We knew we had the ancestors, and we talked to them all of the time. Many times they answered back by thought, and it was rather a given that this would happen. It was not thought of as weird, not thought of as make-believe. Our people were in Truth. There were no lies, so if a youngster told about hearing one of the ancestors, everyone respectably would listen. They would then make comments if need be.

Therefore, when an inquisitive youngster decided to take off on his own, he knew he could find food in the forest, could find water. He knew what berries to eat, what vegetation to chew on. This was not a problem. He just wanted to know what was over the next hill.

Keep in mind that, since he was a giant-child, when he walked, he took long strides. Consequently, he traveled over a great deal of land in one day. As he traveled, he saw different plants and berries. He would try those. He saw hills that he did not know were there. He saw mountains that he did not know were there. He came to waterfalls and marveled at the beauty of the water cascading down.

He automatically knew how to swim so he would dive into pools of water that were so inviting to swim in and so delicious to drink. The water was pure. He did not have to worry about harmful bacteria being in the water. The thought was not even in his memory banks.

The youngster walked and walked. He talked to the animals and scratched some of them behind their ears. He talked to the ancestors. He was in his own world but at the same time walking his real world. After he had walked a bit and had seen some of the sights, he made his way back home, greeted people and then rested.

The next day he said his goodbyes and set off again to explore. His mother gave him a hug and sent him on his way. This time he stayed for two days. The next time he stayed away for three days. Each time he would go further and further away from home.

On one of those journeys, he came to an area that astounded him. At first, there seemed to be a shimmering village he could see in the distance. When he got to it, he saw that it was different, compared to the village he had grown up in. Everything seemed to shimmer. The buildings were different. The dress code was different. Colors were different. Everything was different! For you readers, it would be similar to taking a journey to Peru, perhaps, and seeing the colorful clothing the people wore.

He explored the shimmering village and spoke to the people. They spoke in a language he did not understand. He found this to be very strange, for he thought everyone spoke the same language. Intrigued by all the newness, he stayed with them and learned their way of thinking and doing—their philosophy. He found it was different from his own. They seemed to speak on a different level. They spoke on deep spiritual matters. He had not heard of this. He did not realize that there was another way of being. They had great independence also. Each one seemed to love his or her neighbor but was not dependent upon that one either.

He saw new inventions—new ways of communicating, new ways of transporting oneself, ways of working with the mind to get from one place to another. He saw people at labor who were not slaves. There were no slaves on our planet. Each person worked at a task he or she enjoyed. They worked because they wanted to.

They had great independence. No one told them what to do: *make that; build that; create that.* They worked because they wanted to. Their creative juices would flow. The youth watched this and marveled at it all. He learned many things. He learned about the stars and the heavens—that there were other worlds out there that were totally different from his. He marveled at this.

Since there was no greed in his heart, he had no longing to take anything from them. He admired the beautiful stones he saw but had no desire to take any. It never occurred to him; they were not his and he felt no compunction to take anything that was not his. Therefore, even that was part of his independence—no desire to covet.

When people steal from others, is that not dependency—to steal someone else's beautiful things, is that not dependency? **If you are independent, you can admire a beautiful artifact but have no desire to own it**. It is not yours, so therefore, you do not want it.

This could be a new thought for you readers. **Those who steal**, covet something that is not theirs, **are not independent, but dependent—co-dependent**. This book is on NOW energy, and **dependency is not NOW energy**.

The youth saw many marvels from this new community. He was in awe, for he started to realize how little he really knew— that there were people and places outside of his village who knew differently from his village. Therefore, he felt compelled to return home to tell them of the wonders he had seen. However, what he did not realize was even as he was learning all of this, he also had started his purpose.

He would be known as the *Wanderer*, for that was his purpose—to wander the world—to seek new knowledge and then bring it back to people. Of course there were no newspapers, television and so forth, so this would become part of our oral history—someone who had actually seen and spoken Truth of what his experiences were came back and described all that he had seen. In that way, other villages would learn what was out there. There were other languages, different philosophies, and yet they would and could maintain their independence, for they did not covet any of the new wonders that the Wanderer described.

That could be a lesson for all countries—to visit each other and allow those people to retain their culture and not think because one country has a particular resource that we must have that also. *That country harvests that way; we must show them how to harvest a better way—our way is always better.* There was none of that. Each one was independent. No one coveted his neighbors' possessions, whether it was next door, or the next village, or across the world. No one coveted another person's belongings or way of living.

Therefore, many children, as they grew and matured, became Wanderers. There is that term a *wanderer's lust*—they lust for learning new ways; they lust for seeing what is different out there. *It is not that I want change, but what is different? I just want to know.*

A Wanderer, full of knowledge, full of Light, and full of the NOW energy doing nothing but walking, traveling, seeing, speaking but in total peace, total allowance, total acceptance and a total love for the people and the animals, the mountains, and the waters that he saw. A Wanderer is most likely in the NOW energy if he does not feel the urge to pick up and carry off even a pebble as he walks away from the ocean side. It is not his; it is the ocean's.

I leave you now, readers—another story on your 4th of July, a story of independence of another kind. For NOW energy is independent; it is not co-dependent. Even though everyone is one in the oneness and souls bask in the NOW energy when they go back to the Father, they are still independent. When they feel that tug from their string of consciousness that it is time to come out and move on to another adventure, there is independence. They do not have to ask God's, the Creator's assent. They merely can leave with gratitude and love and go forth on their next journey.

Independence allows you to be without judgment; it allows you to hold *love* so others may feel it.

I AM the Master Jonas and I greet you. *Thank you, Lord.* You are welcome, dear one—you who carried the wonder-lust in your youth and visited many countries, admiring the people, attempting to learn their languages, although you did not succeed fully, but basking in the differences and really enjoying that. You left a trail behind you of people who fondly remember you—all the countries and peoples you met are in your memory banks, for you had and you carried great independence at that time.

All right dear one, that's chapter 17—The Wanderer! Yep (chuckles), been there; done that; that's for sure. *'til we meet again, dear one, I AM Jeshua ben Joseph.*

18

LADY NADA—ROSA

Hello dearest one, I am back once again; I AM Lady Nada. *Oh, Lady Nada, it's so much fun to have you come back; thank you.* It is fun for me to be here, actually. So what do I want to talk about today? Each time we come in with a little bit different story and ideas to suggest to the readers. I think I will just let the story unfold and name it as it goes along.

I do like the phrase authors use to begin a story: *once upon a time*; so I am going say, once upon a time there was a sweet young child who grew to adulthood. She was beautiful to behold, inside and out. She was greatly respected and greatly revered in her family and in her community. Where she lived was larger than a village and yet not what one would call a *city*. This takes place in what you would call the Middle East, where women had a difficult time in showing who they were—having a brain, having intelligence and not being just a sex object.

We will call our lovely woman, *Rosa*. I like that name simply because it reminds me of the beautiful roses that the Mother Mary brought to the planet. So Rosa shall be her name (*and the title of this chapter*).

Rosa did not always have the respect of her family. Again, as I have said, in that Middle Eastern culture, that area, the ole-time-religion was very ripe and present. The patriarchs were not going to let go of their old belief systems very easily. They liked the idea of having the women be utterly subservient to the men's demands and wishes. There were so many laws that kept the women as the lesser god. They had to be heavily veiled where only the eyes looked out, simply because they needed to see where they were going. If one thinks about it, it is somewhat silly to completely cover a woman so only the husband and other male relatives could look upon her. We find that narcissistic and selfish and ever so degrading to the woman.

Therefore, here was this beautiful little child who, when she reached puberty, the age of when young girls became women, was heavily veiled in her *burqa*. She knew that this was what she had to look forward to. She felt repulsion deep inside of her—*if only I could go out and not wear my veils.*

She noticed that on occasion foreign women would come to visit. While they respected the tradition of burqas, they did not dress all veiled. They wore short sleeves; they wore sunglasses to cover their eyes; they wore hats against the sun; they wore sandals and as little clothing as they could get away with because of the heat.

Rosa looked upon these foreign women and envied the freedom they had. The women thought nothing of it as they strode through the bazaars, buying this and that. They even smoked a cigarette in public. They were completely comfortable in their own skin. They seemed to have no compelling desire to please the males, although they could be holding hands with their lover or husband. They walked by the side of their men, sometimes putting their arms around them, just enjoying their togetherness, and not paying any particular attention to those around them.

Rosa envied that freedom. In her prayers she would ask, *please give me more freedom; please send me help in releasing the burden I feel pressing upon me. I do not want to wear these oppressive veils and gowns—everything in black. I want colors; I want to feel the sunshine on my uncovered head. I do not want to be veiled.*

She thought about little else. The household would merely comment on how quiet she was. *Isn't it wonderful; she is so quiet and non-disturbing? The men will not be disturbed by her presence*—although there were men who covertly eyed her and thought about what a lush little piece of fruit she would be as she matures.

Many men traveled to different countries and saw how the European women dressed and acted. While they did not allow their women to act like that, they thoroughly enjoyed being among these liberated strangers.

Rosa attended a school that, of course, was just for the women. They were taught subjects that befitted women. They were never taught what the men studied. The men studied the history of adventurous countries; what was available; what were the resources; what was the government like. Women were taught none of these subjects. It was reasoned, *they do not need to know that. What would they do with such information?* Never once did they think about the fact that one of the young girls would have a searching mind. She would be searching for different ideas, different philosophies, outside of the box that she had been put in.

So the years went by and Rosa rebelled somewhat but was then severely punished at home. She was actually whipped. And of course she was always whipped by a man—her father at that point. If you had a young girl in your family who was a bit precocious, the males always perceived it as a sexual come-on that needed to be squashed. Therefore, Rosa and other female members of the family would be severely punished if they did not follow the rules, toe the line, rarely be seen, and even more, rarely be heard.

However, the Universe had a different purpose for Rosa. Her inner spiritual teachers and guides saw her potential; saw her beauty; noted her intelligence and knew that she had a purpose, that she had a journey that was uniquely hers and different from the other women in the village. Rosa was to mature and not marry early. She was to keep her virginity, of course, to keep her pureness, but she was to feed her mind.

Therefore, she sought to go forward with her schooling, to go to University. Again this was considered an outrageous request and out of the box. However, the Universe had other plans, as it will for you readers, if you will only be open to them.

A contest was provided by some very wealthy visiting dignitaries. They were looking for some bright minds to work in their companies and advance their profits—reaping great rewards. Therefore, they created this testing of young adults. If they passed the test at a high enough level, they would be sent to a respected university all expenses paid and taught ways of the outside world. Anyone could apply. Therefore, Rosa, unbeknownst to her family, applied. She thought *what the heck; I have nothing to lose. If I do not pass, my family will not know of it anyway. I so want to travel; I so want to see outside of my town.*

On the day of the testing, she told her family she needed some things at the market and dashed out heavily veiled with her basket. She passed her family's surveillance. *She's just going to the market; she will be right back.*

She fled to where the testing was, set her basket aside but kept her veils in place. She received the booklet of questions. When she was given the go-ahead, she quickly went through all of the questions. She answered every single one of them. The questions on the map she really did not know, but she found them the easiest to answer, for she just guessed at these geographical questions. She then turned in her booklet and left an address so that the results would not come to her family, but to her friend who she had confided in.

Sure enough, after a few weeks, her friend very excitedly told her that a letter had come from the testing organization she was interested in. Rosa could hardly wait to get through all of the chores that were expected of her and then slip away to her friend's house and read the letter. She was shocked when she read her letter.

You have been accepted into our program, for your entry was one of the highest we received. We look forward to meeting you and your parents. Rosa was ecstatic. She never knew that she could do what she did, take a test, finish it and be the highest one. Then her elation fell, for she knew she would have to tell her father. She was afraid of him and his wrath. However, she had come too far to stop now. What she did not know was that her angels and guides were prodding her to give the letter to her father when he was alone, then to wait quietly for his reaction. It so happened that Rosa's father had a modest income but his expectation was to marry Rosa to a wealthy man. It would be nice if the man were young, but most likely he would be an older gentleman with a well-established income—perhaps a widower who needed a wife. The marriages were always arranged to the benefit of the father and not particularly to the benefit of the bride-to-be. Female children were raised that this was their destiny. They had seen their own sisters marry. Rarely had one of them married for love. And before one knew it, here would come an older man who was set in his ways. He usually was not that attractive nor had he kept his body young and virile.

Rosa knew what her destiny would be like, so she gave the letter to her father and stood there respectfully with her head lowered but with raised eyes so she could watch his expression. At first, the father did not know what to expect when she handed him the letter. He thought that maybe it was a proposal of marriage, for we must remember, reader, that was all that he had on his mind at that time—to turn his daughter into a commodity. Let her marry a man who would bring him wealth. That was where his true feelings lay.

He opened the letter happily, thinking he was going to read a proposal, and instead he read how the officials praised Rosa for her brilliant entry to their contest—an entry that would allow her to go to the University, all expenses paid, and be given an allowance as compensation to the father for the loss of his daughter. These officials were very wise and knew that if they were going to seek new people for the growth of their companies that some of the employees could be women. And if they were women—they were not going to make their decision based on gender—but if the winner were a woman, they were well aware that they would have to compensate the father. He would probably get so much money from a suitor, so they matched that. He saw the amount of money, which was actually more than any suitors would have offered. He was told what a brilliant mind Rosa had and what a brilliant future she would have with this company if she would but go through the University and graduate first.

The father was so shocked that he forgot his pattern of hemming and hawing, lighting his pipe, and getting out his strap in order to beat her. He just stood and stared at the letter, then stared at her and sputtered, drank more tea. Finally, he exclaimed, *Rosa, did you dare defy me and go and take this test; don't you see how you shamed me?* Everything revolved around him in his world, so for Rosa to do this without his permission, it boggled his mind.

Rosa kept respectfully silent. She knew when to speak and when not to speak in that family. She let him unwind as he read and re-read the letter. After many a—hems and grunts of displeasure, he told Rosa that they would go at the appointed time and check out the authenticity of the offer; check out the offices and even check out the University.

Therefore, on the appointed date, Rosa put on her veils—the black burqa that covered her. They went to see the officials who knew the ways of that country. They treated the father with great courtesy and respect, gave them comfortable chairs to sit in and served tea. Several of the officials came into the room to talk to him; then they turned and talked to Rosa, and then they turned and talked to him some more. Before he knew it, they were all conversing and taking part in the conversation. Instead of having to stay quiet and say nothing, Rosa was able to voice her opinions, answer their questions, to ask her father for his opinion. He was so caught up in the dynamic going on that he started treating her almost as if she were an equal and not just his daughter. When all the negotiations had been voiced, he signed his approval, making more of an X versus a signature, while Rosa wrote out her name in a cursive style.

Rosa was given a woman mentor who was not of her religion, not of her heritage, but one who was more worldly. This woman taught Rosa the ways of the world—a clean, refined view. Rosa graduated from University with honors. She was given a position in the company and became a respected business woman who was not only honored in the community, but also honored in her family.

Rosa brought gifts for her family, and she helped them make changes for the better. She did marry, but she married a man of her choosing and a man whom she loved. But that is another story.

We will leave Rosa now, but the object of this story, readers, was to emphasize for you that just because you were born into a family with a certain culture, certain religious trainings, that you should listen to your inner guidance. Is this for you? Is this what you came to do? If you are feeling rebellious in a spiritual way, in an appropriate way, then go on with your divine guidance. It is your journey and only you can make that journey. You do not make it for someone else just to please him or her. You make the journey because it is your soul's plan for you. It is the Universe's destiny-plan for you. We hope you will listen with an open heart.

I AM Lady Nada, and I greet you this morning. Adieu.

Thank you Lady Nada, it is a reflective story.

It is sad to know that such a story is still true today—the heavy veils, the heavy tradition, the heavy culture needs to be lessened. It needs to change and to have its veils dropped here and there.

Blessings . . .

All right, dear one, you did it. *Yes, it seemed to flow easier.* Yes, it did; keep at it for we are not through yet! I AM Jeshua ben Joseph.

19

FATHER-MOTHER GOD—YOUTH

Hello, My precious daughter, I AM your Father. *Ah, I was wondering if you were going to give me a little story similar to what the others have been doing.* But of course, I am not going to miss this opportunity. So with that being said, let Me start My little story. I have delighted in all of these stories that the various Presenters have given you.

As I look upon this little boy child in My story, I realize that he did not have much going for him in his lifetime. When his parents conceived him, they were not consciously aware they were doing that. They were in their addictions—much drinking, some dope. They had no idea they were creating a baby's body for this magnificent soul to come into.

Interestingly enough, the way the angels handled this was for the mother to have quite violent morning sickness. The only foods she could keep down in her stomach were nourishing things. She could keep down a banana for the fruit. She could keep down a piece of fresh fish. Her body could not tolerate anything fried.

Just the smell of it or of coffee would make her ill. She actually nourished her body in quite a healthy way. She knew that drugs would be harmful for a baby, so she abstained from them. She wished at times she could have had a nice liquored drink, but she soon realized that when she did not drink, she was not sick.

Her husband continued on his downward spiral with liquor, drugs, and other women. But she started to concentrate on the fact that she had this baby growing inside of her. She had never owned anything, never had anything that was totally hers. There were other siblings in her family, and if one had a sweater, one sister would take that sweater and wear it without asking. They would just take each other's clothes, wear each other's simple rings or bracelets and never tell each other what they were doing. So you can see, the boundaries were very weak for this family.

The months passed and it was the time she would be going into labor. She knew of a midwife who people in her economic situation would use to deliver their babies. In that way, she would not have the expense of a hospital and doctors. She had a successful delivery, and the baby was a precious little boy.

His mother's heart opened, and she gave the child all the love that she was capable of giving. She had a low paying job, but she managed to buy what her son needed. She sent him to her church school, for they took in charity students. The lad had schooling: he learned his A, B, Cs, learned how to write his name, learned how to do sums, but what surprised everyone was that he started being drawn to music. He would sit up and take notice whenever he heard a tune being played on the piano on TV. Later he would sneak into the church, for there was a rec room with an old piano. He would sit at that piano and pick out tunes. He was able to spread his fingers so that he was soon playing chords and moving his fingers up and down the keys.

He was what one would call a *child prodigy* in music. He could not read any music, but he merely heard it and could play anything that he heard. The music seemed to flow into his ears and out his hands. There was always a need for someone to play a piano at the church functions. He gladly sat there for hours playing anything that anyone requested. He enjoyed the food and sweets that he was given. He always had a plate on top of the piano with snacks and sandwiches and cookies. There was a glass of milk or lemonade—church fare, but it was wholesome and usually homemade.

Therefore, when he went home at night to his one room, an attic in someone's house, he was actually full. He had eaten pieces of salami, the little weenies, chicken legs, raw vegetables, and desserts. He always went home well fed. He was even able to bring some of the food home with him—quartered oranges. He could hold those over until morning. When he got up in the morning, he would have his oranges and the leftover cookies and anything else that he had brought that did not need refrigeration.

Along with this prodigy's talents, he had ambition. He just knew that he was directed. Everything seemed to fall into place for him. If he had a wish for something, it would occur. He started to recognize this. He started to realize that he was not making this happen. He was being looked after by his guardian angels. He truly believed this. Since he was associated with a church, he believed in the Saints and the Lords. He wore a crude necklace around his neck with a cross on it—one that he had found when someone had tossed it aside because the thong holding the cross was frayed. The cross was not real metal. He always found everything that he wanted. He had no compunction about accepting what one would call *second hand* or *hand-me-downs*, for he knew that once he had it, it would be his—he never thought about the fact that he was wearing someone else's clothes. They were now just his.

One day when he was in the rec room by himself, tickling the keys, as we put it, a stranger stood in the doorway and listened. He was drawn to the ability of this young lad. He recognized the prodigy in this boy. The man was very wealthy and very well known in the field of music, in the field of concerts, in the field of movies.

He went to the pastor of the church and asked if there were any restrictions about taking this child as his protégé to teach him the ways of the music world, teach him the ways of the artists. The pastor told him that the youth's parents were no longer living. They had overdosed on drugs, actually, and had given up their obligations to the child several years ago. The church had put the child under its wing, so to speak, and was watching out for him.

The man, a great artist and producer himself, took the youth who was rapidly becoming a young man. He gave him a mentor, and under the mentor's tutelage, the boy was taught the manners of society. He was shown how to be clean—to be clean in his person, to wear clean clothes. He was shown what clothes were appropriate to wear for his age and abilities. He was led into the world of stardom.

Now readers, the object of my story is to emphasize the fact that children usually do not know in their heads their purpose. They have an inner knowing and that is in their heart. They just know what they have a passion for and they go after it. They will not put up roadblocks, for they do not imagine they cannot have what they want. They came in with the idea that anything they want can be obtained with hard work and dedication. The lad learned this early in his life. He knew his Truth. He knew when people were lying to him or just wanted something from him. He could just feel it. He did not have the words for this. He did not know the words for this dynamic—all those esoteric terms. He just knew in his heart that that person was not in Truth, or that person was lying to him, or that person really liked him in an honorable way.

Therefore, he grew to be very successful in his life. While he had some champagne perhaps after his performances, he rarely drank on his own. He did not smoke because he did not like the fact that his fingers could become stained. He was very meticulous about keeping his hands and fingers perfect so that he could play. His nails were always trimmed.

As he got older, women of all demeanors followed him, fawned over him. There was one woman who caught his eye. Of course, she was the one he had a contract with before they were born. He recognized her, not from that esoteric position but from the fact that there was something about her he was drawn to. Of course, they fell in love and his life became like a fairytale—they fell in love, had children, and had a beautiful, loving life. It was an exciting life with all the artists and what are called the *beautiful people* that he met.

The story I am telling you does not bring in any of the dark, the nether-lands that many people are drawn to—the dark side, We will say. You have read about and have seen in movies where this wonderful artist starts drinking too much, using drugs too much, abusing the body with the addictions. And then he loses everything—even sometimes taking his or life at the end.

The story I am bringing you is about the opposite choice, the one you can have if you follow your heart. Your heart will never lead you astray. You follow your heart and you follow your passion of doing, of taking action. You are in the NOW energy when you are playing your piano. It is running through your fingers as you sway to the music. You are in that zone of the NOW.

It is a wonderful place to be, dear readers. It is a wonderful place to strive for attainment. Attainment is possible; attainment will happen when your soul is ready, when it knows without a doubt the lessons that it had come to learn. It will know and it will guide the body to stardom if the personality in the body will just listen.

I AM your Father-Mother God, dear readers. I know all your thoughts; I know all your prayers. And remember, I give you free will so that it is entirely up to you—your choice on to stardom on a soul level into higher dimensions; or is it going to lead you to the nether-land, slipping and sliding down where the distortions and the discord prevail?

I bless you, My children; I love you unconditionally; I love you. *Thank you, Father, that was wonderful.* And you, My child, are doing so well. I AM just delighted in you and in your efforts to keep going in your advancement to know Me even more. I thank you.

20

ARCHANGEL MICHAEL—INDIAN

Archangel Michael reminisces: We are working with the NOW energy. We have told you that the NOW is one of *Peace, Contentment, Joy, Action With No Action*. In one of our books, I gave you the true story of a soldier in war where it is drilled to kill or be killed. The soldiers had a choice at that moment: run for their lives or to stay, give battle and kill the enemy. Or, if they wished not to kill, to accept their decision or choice to be killed— NOW energy. This morning as you, our dear channel, sit in your bedroom alcove listening to the life-giving rain pattering past your windows, the Earth drinks it in. In Arizona, rain is prayed for and is gratefully received when it comes.

There were times that this state that you live in was populated by the Indians. They would perform the rain dances. Unbeknownst to you perhaps, you have a Monad who sent out fingers of consciousness as an Indian child. You grew up and taught the Indians their ceremonial dances. You have heard this before and all is true.

So my story is about an Indian child whose name was *He Who Brings Rain*. In this child's camp were the Shamans who taught the people to dance for rain. However, this one season, it seemed as if the Great Spirits were not listening. The Shamans knew that something was amiss. They knew there was an element that was not being incorporated. They did not know what it was. They tried different methods for calling in the rain. They shook their gourds; they stomped their feet in a rhythmic way. They gathered the people and had them chant different words. But still, the rain did not come. The Shamans prayed to the Great Spirits asking for guidance. *What do you want us to do? What are we missing here? What do you need in order to bring us rain?* There was only a single response: *let it unfold; continue your dancing and let it unfold.*

Therefore, day after day the tribe would rest up and when it was cooler in the evening, they danced and they danced. They took turns, for they were dancing almost to exhaustion. They then would go to bed. They would lie with their woman thinking that perhaps in this pro-creation, she would help bring in the rain, but nothing happened.

One night, as the tribe had danced to near exhaustion and they were just laying where they fell, a young boy, a toddler really, came out of his tent seeking his mother for he was hungry. He wanted her nourishment. He wanted her breast and the succulent milk. He noticed the tribe was sprawled in a circle, so he entered it and wandered from one person to another looking for his mother. Then as children do, he started stomping his feet. Sounds came out of his mouth and he stomped more. He wailed and he stomped even more, searching for his mother.

While he stomped his feet, large drops of rain started to fall. At first the drops only fell on the young toddler and seemed to follow him like a shadow as he stomped his feet going around the circle seeking his mother's nurturing succulence. He was rather amazed and put his head back, opened his mouth, and stuck out his tongue so that this rain could give him drops of water. The drops were large and fat and full of water. They felt good as they popped open on his tongue. Before the tribe knew it, they were sitting in a downpour of rain. It rained and it rained. Everyone basked in the rain and gave thanks to the Spirits and then went off to their teepees.

The mother found her wandering son, her errant son, and swept him up in her arms with joy because everyone was happy with the rain. She took him back into their tent and fed him. Soon the rain stopped. Everyone was asleep by then, but since the ground was so parched, the water soon disappeared into the dry cracks.

Therefore, the next morning when they arose, it was like it had never rained. So the chief called for another rain dance. *We will do it again; we will have it again in the cooler evening hours.* Again they danced and stomped their feet but nothing happened. However, this time the little boy, who was sitting with his mother after she had danced, got up, thinking it was a game. He ran into the circle and whooped and copied what the tribe had been doing by stomping his feet. Then he stood in the middle of the circle and raised his arms with his head thrown back and the rains would come. Each night it was the same until the tribe realized that this little boy, this little warrior, was the bringer of rain.

The chiefs, the Shamans, laid their hands and feathers on the toddler's head and named him *He Who Brings Rain.* As the toddler grew to a young man, he was called into service, service to other tribes. *Come to our area, you who bring the rain. Let's get* He Who Brings Rain *to come to us so that we may have rain also.* Therefore, he was the traveling Rain-man and wherever he went and danced, the rain would come. It could be a clear night and yet after he danced and whooped and hollered, the clouds would gather and the rain would come.

Readers, you might be wondering why this would be an example of NOW energy. It was action with no action, for the dancing was gratitude and joy; it was thanks and *please, Great*

Spirit, honor us with rain. Many people move their bodies when they pray. The *Whirling Dervishes* are an example. People dance and move many times when they pray to God and as the energy comes through their bodies. So it is still action without action, for it is bodies moving from the energy of deep gratitude. This is a different example of NOW energy, for the movement is still called no action; you are moving to the Creator's energies, swaying, calling forth the Great Spirit for help. That is still action with no action.

This story also depicts the fact that the elders could only see it one way and did not realize that the gift that they were asking for lay fallow in the smallest person, the youngest person, the toddler, who was greatly connected to the Great Spirit.

Do not, dear readers, shun the young people as not having the wisdom or not knowing, for the gift you may be seeking many times is in these newer bodies. They do not have the heavy veils over them. They are more pure in that the density of humanity has not settled in yet. Your schools need to change, for they are still trying to teach in a 3D way to 5D bodies. It does not work and will not work.

It is rather amusing, dear readers, for as this channel sits here listening to the rain and to my thoughts, there is a happy woodpecker pecking away on the outer boards—the sounds of Nature. The channel sits here with a smile on her face. Her senses are alive as she takes all of this in simultaneously.

I AM Archangel Michael; call upon me and I will come. You may not know what is needed to help you to the next level, but I see it clearly and I will come and help. I am but a thought away. I bless you, my children. I AM Archangel Michael.

Thank you, Archangel Michael; it is a lovely story. You are welcome, dear one. All for now.

21

MASTER JONAS—DOUBT

Good morning everyone; I am one of the off-world Beings, one of the Giants. My tale is a little different from what you may be expecting, for our lessons are different from yours. You as human Beings take on the lessons of ego: how not to be in greed, how to communicate, how to have relationships. On my planet, the lessons are how to serve others, how to be in the NOW, how to give. So I will start with this story. And as most stories start, we'll take a child and have that child progress through his different steps of development. We have already told you about one young man who was a Wanderer. This is another story about a young lad. He would probably be around six or seven in your terms.

From the moment he had consciousness, he felt that he had a great purpose in store, but he did not know what it was. The adults around him assured him that when it was the correct time, he would know; his Higher Teachers would tell him what to do and when to do it.

He also was a Wanderer and would visit different villages on our planet. He would see that where he thought there would be happiness, some people were not happy. They were not in joy. He did not understand this, for he was led to believe that if you stayed in the heart and did not judge your neighbor that your life would be happy.

He started thinking about this. As he advanced in his formative years, he noticed other things about his neighbors and the people in different villages that he visited. Some were argumentative. He felt it was not an exchange of ideas, but a demand that the person think the other person's way. And this puzzled him.

He felt that there was something lacking in the person's training. Or something was interfering where the person was not receiving correct information. It bothered him. He went to the village Elder, some might call him a shaman or a priest in a nonreligious way, and he asked what was wrong here; what was holding up the advancement in consciousness for these people?

He started to feel the emotion. Oh, he said, they doubt their own ability. Oh, he said, they are forgetting who they are; they are forgetting that they have come from Source. He knew this with all of his Being. He told his Elder of his revelation, and the Elder validated that this was true. The Elder said that even on this great planet of ours, even on a planet such as ours of high consciousness, you will find people who doubt their own abilities.

Now it is true that there could be peer pressure; there could be parenting involved. But our young lad, who we will call the *Seeker*, knew something had caused these highly-evolved people to stagnate as their doubts of themselves grew stronger. They started to doubt their own abilities—their own abilities to be at higher levels—higher levels in education, higher levels in social adjustments, higher levels in teaching, higher levels in spirituality. It kept them from reaching goals that they had set for themselves.

Our seeker wondered and asked his Elder, how does this get turned around? How can people break through this blockage of doubt? The Elder explained that many times when a blockage occurs as strong as these people are experiencing, when it is that strong, something will occur in their daily life that they will have to confront. It can be a simple event. Maybe a person will be called upon to give a presentation, and this person doubts his ability to do so. Maybe the person's Higher Self told him that something wonderful was going to happen, and then it did not happen.

When this occurred, the shock itself changed the vibration. It changed the frequency around the person so that adjustments could be made. Adjustments could be made in all areas—mental, emotional, and physical—for the shock of the event reverberated deeply throughout that person's system. It was up to the person to rebalance, to recognize where the resulting anger was pointed, and to know that the anger was pointed at himself or herself, to recognize that the person created that in some way so that the adjustments could be made.

In the consciousness of Beings that are more evolved and more advanced, while they may have these moments or episodes of imbalance, they learn to draw upon their wisdom. They learn how to adjust, how to rebalance . . .

Author: it was at this point that I received a phone call. I waited for the message machine to click off, but after listening to the message, I came out of trance and knew I could not continue. (A client was telling me that her check to me for a reading had been stolen and the thief had cashed it in Missouri. LOL!)

A few days later, Jeshua said to go with what was already said by Master Jonas and emphasize to the readers how doubt can become a major block for people. Therefore, readers, think back when you have been stuck on something and have not gone forward with your project. Had doubt of your ability crept in? If you feel emotion as you think about this, know that you already know the answer to this in your heart. But remember, there is no room for doubt when you are in the NOW energy zone.

Doubt is a judgment about something. It is frequently used in our English language: Oh, I doubt that! *That word needs to be taken out of "the library of your mind," for each time it is uttered, a judgment has been made. And that makes the NOW inaccessible.*

22

SAINT GERMAIN—PRINCE

Good morning, dear one. As you know, I, Saint Germain, had lives in the courts of royalty. I spent much time in court, so I was a part of the royals' lives. I was mainly interested in how the children were being raised. You have heard the horror stories where a baby or young prince was killed so the next in line could be able to advance.

In the court that I frequented, there was a dear little boy who would often be dressed in blue velvets. The child found them cumbersome, and he was forever taking off his hat or taking off his jacket. Since he did not have the dexterity or patience to unbutton his jacket, he just ripped it off. The buttons were always flying throughout the various rooms. He preferred just running around in his nightshirt, but that was not allowed outside of his nursery.

One day after the nurse had dressed him in his velvets and led him by hand to join the others, the child started rebelling. The young prince knew how to throw a temper tantrum to get his way. He discovered that if he just sat down on the floor, that also would give him his way. They could not budge him. Sometimes he was angrily pulled by the collar by one of the matrons.

On one particular day after the nurse had left him in the room with a crowd of people, he was getting too warm. Children have their natural heat, and he was getting warm and prickly. The ruffled collars made his neck itch until finally he just yanked his jacket open, and the buttons went flying off as he struggled out of the coat. He noticed his long stockings were also uncomfortable. It was just too hot. There was no air conditioning in those days, so he sat on the floor and pulled his stockings off. His feet felt so free that he refused to put his shoes back on.

So there he sat in his undergarment, his fancy blue velvet pants that came down to the knee with no stockings and no shoes. He then got up and started running through the court. Most of the people, the royals, were used to seeing him and his antics. They grumbled, but when the little prince was happy, they were happy. When he was throwing his tantrums, everyone was uncomfortable. Consequently, it was just easier on everyone to let the child run around half-dressed. They labeled him as being sort of weak in the mind, and that label allowed him to get away with his rebellions.

One day, a little princess came to visit. He was all dressed in his velvets, again squirming, waiting until he could be in the anterooms to pluck off his jacket. However, when he saw the little princess and how perfectly she was dressed, he did not want to appear less in her eyes. He wanted her to like him and not think of him as being addlebrained, so he kept his clothes on.

She had come with her parents who were going to visit for quite a while. Therefore, the prince and the little princess became good friends. They were given free rein in the palace and out in the courtyards. They were soon running hither and yon, exploring this and exploring that. He showed her his favorite spots to hide so they could spy on the other people in the rooms. They ran and played and went to the stables and hid in the haystacks and watched the grooms care for the horses. They had such a good time, for they were being allowed to just be children.

Readers, if you are a child and are reading this book or another is reading it to you, be aware that children can be in the NOW. In fact, many times children are closer to being in the NOW than their adult family members, teachers and/or friends. Why is this so? It is because of their innocence. They do not yet know the negativity of the world. They do not know the different ideologies of religions, the belief systems of others that could press in upon them.

They are in their own world. In their world they do not think of killings and rapes and harming others. They can just sit in a corner and go inward to their world. Some call it fantasy, but they are happy there. And most likely, they are closer to Source at those times. They are in the NOW, feeling contentment, especially if they have had a good meal. They feel content.

Therefore, these two small royals in their innocence could play and take pleasure in being children. There were no sexual games between them since they had not reached that age of development. You have seen where puppy dogs play with each other—just taking enjoyment in each other's company. Then, once they are sleepy, they just lean on each other and doze off. That is the NOW.

Children, this is a message for you. Keep your heart open and uncluttered; keep your belief in your God, your Source; ask often for the Angels to guide and help you, no matter how crazy or stupid it may sound to others who tell you Angels do not exist. Angels are very much present, and they are always willing to help as soon as you ask, but you must always ask first. You need not go to anyone in particular. Your religions say you have to go to the priest or pastor or someone in that capacity. That is not Truth. You do not have to do that; you merely ask with your thoughts, *Angels help me; Angels help me find this; Angels guide me to this.* Many adults ask Angels to help them find a parking place, and lo and behold, a parking place opens up. A person pulls out of a spot just as they wish to pull in.

Our little royals learned to play with each other and they learned to rely upon each other, for they knew the other would speak Truth to them. There was no reason to lie. They knew that when they asked something of their friend that Truth would be spoken. When the little prince told the little princess how he struggled with all his clothes, she giggled and said that she too had trouble. She told him that the gowns had so many undergarments—petticoats—and were so heavy. They were hot and scratched her. She was always relieved when at nighttime she could take them off and get ready for bed. The little prince would agree. *I too am so glad when I can shed these clothes!*

So, dear readers, the *shedding of clothes* can be used in many metaphors, can they not? As you mature, do you not shed ideas that no longer work for you? You shed clothes and buy new ones so you can be wearing a similar fashion that your peers wear. You shed your belief systems. Therefore, *shedding* is a metaphor for many things and a great enabler for the NOW energy to come in.

I AM Saint Germain dear ones; bless you.

CONCLUSION—JESHUA

Dear readers, we are drawing the conclusion to this little book. While you hold the book in your hands, it might seem quite simple, but for those of you who have read our books over the years, you know that *simple* many times reads *profound*. The energy in this book is very strong—the NOW energy. When you hold this book in your hands— some sleep with the books under their pillow—and especially when you say the Dedication out loud, that is NOW energy.

At first, that energy seemed nebulous to you; it did not mean much. It was a word that people did not understand and do not understand even today. However, it packs quite a wallop and has become so important. More and more authors are writing about being in the NOW. It becomes the on-going theme for many—not only for authors, but also for Lightworkers. The Lightworkers talk about whether they are in the NOW energy or not, whether they are in present time. Are they here and NOW? Are their thoughts loving? That becomes a guidepost for you.

As soon as your thought turns negative, turns judgmental, or becomes distorted, you have left the NOW. At one time, on a soul level, you basked in the NOW energy for thousands and millions of years at a time; and YES, you are that old. People talk about their past lives. They have had so many of them that they tend to forget what they did in past lives on this planet and on other planets. Your Starseeds come from different planets. Many of you have your own spaceships. When you read or go to lectures that are futuristic or about New Age thought or are about spaceships, know that you are being drawn to those because they are reflecting memories that you hold. They are reflecting where you have been, where you have lived, and where you still may be going.

There is no end to you. The only beginning is when Source created you. From then on, there is no ending or beginning. Each lifetime leads into another experience. Everything that you do is an experience the soul wishes to know—to gain more expertise in a particular subject. You younger readers, just by joining a sport—whether it is baseball, football, gymnastics, cheerleading, swimming, hockey, polo, or horse shows—all of those experiences happened because your soul chose that journey in order to learn more.

Remember, in this lifetime you are learning things for the first time, but most likely, it is really not the first time. You have played this role before in other lifetimes or on other planets. You just want to hone that experience to make it perfect. Do you think the great musicians, composers like Mozart and Beethoven, just came in this lifetime to learn it all now? No, they came this lifetime and brought that brilliance in from other lifetimes, and then in this lifetime they learned different lessons. Maybe they were not able to handle it emotionally before, so they came back in this lifetime with the same talent as an opportunity to hone the emotions further (Mozart)—to make adjustments.

There are so many different ways to look at a person's life. Therefore, you young readers, as you read about the NOW energy, know that you have had it before. Know that this is not your first experience of the NOW. You are remembering or waking up. It is a dream, an illusion that you are waking up to.

Staying in the NOW, dear reader, is one of the most important lessons being given to you. It is the opportunity to remember what it is like to be in this energy of the NOW, to bask in it, to feel the contentment, with no judgment, just is; what is, is; no action; what is, is. Remember, readers, remember you have done it before. Just remember.

We in the Spiritual Heavenlies look after you. We are all part of the NOW energy. We are all part of each other. I, in my lifetime as Jesus, said to the people of antiquity *what you do unto others, you do unto me.* Since I am part of you, what you do unto others, you do unto yourself! Be kind to yourself; be loving to yourself.

I AM Jeshua ben Joseph, spokesperson for the Heavenlies and advocate of the NOW. We bless you, readers, and we give you our love. Greetings.

All right, dear one, that's it, our little book. Any of your struggles were all part of the learning process. You broke through the block; that's the main thing, and you have now accomplished a pure channeling. All is well, dear one. I suggest we go back to our former way of connecting with each other at 2:00 PM on Saturdays.

Your birthday is coming up, dear one. I have not forgotten this time, so I will give you an advanced Happy, Happy Birthday, my precious love, and many, many more years ahead of you. Do not worry about an aged body, dear one; it is being rejuvenated, although I imagine you doubt that at times. But the Father is certainly aware, as are all the Masters and Angels that work with you. We know that if we want a particular Starseed to continue, there must be miracles for the body. We know.*

So until Saturday, dear one, I AM Jeshua. Thank you so much for everything and this wonderful book, Jeshua!

* Author: I had a body session Friday, August 23, that was a miracle. Jeshua, in the Etheric, came forth and laid his hands over my practitioner's hands. She was telepathically told that her hands were

now his hands and it would be his hands and energy scanning and healing my body. He re-calibrated my brain, took two hands full of grief out of my throat chakra, melted away some plaque build-up in the carotid arteries, removed a poisoned dart with the poison intact from my heart chakra, and made further adjustments throughout my body. As his/her hands scanned my back, he pronounced, "All is well." WOW! What a birthday gift!!

EPILOGUE

Dear readers, I started this book on May 25 and basically finished it on August 22, almost three months. The number 3 is so strong in my life—3 daughters, 3 months to join my military husband in Viet Nam years ago, etcetera.

I cannot say this book flowed effortlessly, especially in chapter 21, but with Jeshua's help, we got it done! The subject of the NOW seems to be timely, for more and more authors and channels are speaking about it. I purposely have not read any of the books and toward the end of my book in August only allowed myself to listen to a CD and an Internet class about the NOW by Kelsey and Brad Wallis. Kelsey trance channels Julius, similar to how Esther Hicks channels Abraham. Julius says *the NOW is virgin territory, never been played out before*. That statement certainly is a good yardstick by which to measure the NOW.

Readers frequently want to know if there is another book in the making. I seem to get themes for my new books and when to start them. So far, I have not been alerted that way. Therefore, I will just sit back and let my Guides, Teachers, and Higher Self decide when to give me a nudge to get back to work on the next book.

I do enjoy hearing from you, so please let me know how you felt about this NOW book. Blessings to all, Chako.

AZCHAKO@AOL.COM
www.Godumentary.com/chako

APPENDIX

JESHUA'S PRAYER

God, bless these words I am hearing and
Let them be the spoken Truth
from your Sons and Daughters of Light.
Send us your protection and keep us in your
Grace,
In the Christ Light, Amen, Amen, Amen.

SANANDA'S IDENTITY COMMAND
By Celestial Blue Star & David of Arcturus circa: 2004

"In the name of Jesus Christ, I now command that if you are not of the highest, most evolved form of Jesus the Christ Consciousness, that you are to here and now disappear immediately and NEVER return."

"I now demand in the name of Jesus the Christ to know if you are a Being of the Jesus the Christ Consciousness; if you are a Being of the true God of the God Light Consciousness of The Creator, answer me yes or no."

"I here and now command in the name of Jesus The Christ that if there is any entity that is not the most evolved form of the Jesus The Christ consciousness, that is not of the most evolved form of God I AM, then you are to here and now disappear and cease to exist. This I command in the name of Jesus The Christ."

ACKNOWLEDGMENTS

It became so clear to me that I would have been lost without the help of my dearest first born, Susan Verling Miller O'Brien and my editor, Heather Clarke. Dear friend, Heather, I thank you so much for all the editing you did in such a timely matter. It kept me keeping on! And Susan, the work you did on framing the book, organizing the Table of Contents, AND coming up with the idea for the cover just boggles my mind. My heart is overflowing.

Jason Smallwood, my grandson of 9 years at the time, provided the photograph of the rainbow over Paradise Island, Nassau, in 2012. The family owns a condo there at The Reefs Hotel, and Jason took the picture from the 17th floor balcony. Little did we know at the time that he would be providing me with the cover for my next book! Thank you so much, Jason. The photo is awesome!

My deepest gratitude and love to Father-Mother God and the many Masters who brought their vignettes forth for our book. Each tale is different and provides the reader another insight of how the NOW is or is not a part of our life.

My love and gratitude I give in abundance to Jeshua. I appreciate so much how he sets a book up, tells me the starting date, and is right there ready to begin when I am. I am so blessed.

This certainly has been a team effort, and I thank one and all for their steadfastness. My love to all of you!

LIST OF PREVIOUS BOOKS

Verling CHAKO Priest, Ph.D.

The Ultimate Experience, the Many Paths to God series:

BOOKS 1, 2, & 3 REVISITED (2011)
ISBN # 978-1-4269-7664-3 (sc)
ISBN# 978-1-4269-7665-0 (e-book)
REALITIES of the CRUCIFIXION (2006)
ISBN # 1-978-4669-2148-1
MESSAGES from the HEAVENLY HOSTS (2007)
ISBN # 1-4251-2550-6
YOUR SPACE BROTHERS and SISTERS GREET YOU! (2008)
ISBN # 978-1-4251-6302-0
TEACHINGS of the MASTERS of LIGHT (2008)
ISBN # 978-1-4251-8573-2
PAULUS of TARSUS (2010)
ISBN # 978-1-4669-209-1 (sc)
ISBN # 978-1-4669-2090-3 (e-book)
THE GODDESS RETURNS to EARTH (2010)
ISBN # 978-1-4269-3563-3

Verling CHAKO Priest, Ph.D.

ISBN # 978-1-4269-3564-0 (e-book)
JESUS: MY BELOVED CONNECTION TO HUMANITY AND
THE SEA Revised Edition (2013)
CO-AUTHOR REV. CYNTHIA WILLIAMS
ISBN # 978-1-4669-7641-2(sc)
ISBN # 978-1-4669-7642-9(hc)
ISBN # 978-1-4669-7640-5(e)
Available at Trafford: 1-888-232-4444
Or, Amazon.com
www.godumentary.com/chako.htm

READER'S NOTES

ABOUT THE AUTHOR

Verling (CHAKO) Priest, PhD was born in Juneau, Alaska, hence her name of Cheechako, shortened to just Chako by her mother, a medical doctor, and her father, an Orthodontist. Chako was raised in Napa, CA. She attended the University of California at Berkeley where she met her future husband. Upon their marriage and after his training as a Navy pilot, they settled into the military way of life. They lived twelve years outside of the United States Mainland in various places, which included Hawaii, Viet Nam, Australia, and Greece. Little did she know that these exotic lands and peoples were preparing her for her spiritual awakening years hence?

After her husband's retirement from the Navy, they resettled in Napa, California. It was during this time that she returned to school at Berkeley, transferred to Sonoma University where she earned her first two degrees in Psychology. Chako then entered the doctoral program at the Institute of Transpersonal Psychology (ITP), renamed Sufi University, which is now located in Palo Alto, CA. She successfully completed that program which consisted of a Master, as well as the Doctorate in Transpersonal Psychology. Ten years and four degrees later she was able to pursue her passion for Metaphysical and New Age Thought—her introduction into the realm of the Spiritual Hierarchy and the Ascended Lords and Masters.

In 1988, Dr. Priest moved to Minnetonka, Minnesota. She co-authored a program called, *Second Time Around* for those with recurring cancer for Methodist Hospital. She, as a volunteer, also facilitated a grief group for Pathways of Minneapolis, and had a private practice.

She studied with a spiritual group in Minnetonka led by Donna Taylor and the Teacher, a group of 5 highly developed entities trance-channeled by Donna. The group traveled extensively all over the world working with the energy grids of the planet and regaining parts of their energies that were still in sacred areas waiting to be reclaimed by them, the owners. They climbed in and out of the pyramids in Egypt, tromped through the Amazon forest in Venezuela, rode camels at Sinai, and climbed the Mountain. Hiked the paths at Qumran, trod the ancient roadways in Petra, Jordan, and walked where the Master Yeshua/Jesus walked in Israel.

The time came, November 1999, when Chako was guided to move to Arizona—her next period of growth. This is where she found her beloved Masters, who in reality had always been with her. They were **all** ready for her next phase, bringing into the physical several books—mind-provoking books, telepathically received by her, from these highly evolved, beautiful, loving Beings. Each book stretches her capabilities, as well as her belief systems. Nevertheless, it is a challenge she gladly embraces.

It is now August, 2013. She has finished writing her eleventh book, about the TALES of NOW. Blessings.

Comments AZCHAKO@AOL.COM.

www.Godumentary.com/chako